A Concise
Introduction
to Microsoft Works

ALSO AVAILABLE

A Concise
Introduction
to Microsoft Works

by
N. Kantaris
and
P.R.M. Oliver

BERNARD BABANI (publishing) LTD.
THE GRAMPIANS
SHEPHERDS BUSH ROAD
LONDON W6 7NF
ENGLAND

PLEASE NOTE

Although every care has been taken with the production of this book to ensure that any projects, designs, modifications and/or programs, etc., contained herewith, operate in a correct and safe manner and also that any components specified are normally available in Great Britain, the Publishers and Author(s) do not accept responsibility in any way for the failure (including fault in design) of any project, design, modification or program to work correctly or to cause damage to any equipment that it may be connected to or used in conjunction with, or in respect of any other damage or injury that may be so caused, nor do the Publishers accept responsibility in any way for the failure to obtain specified components.

Notice is also given that if equipment that is still under warranty is modified in any way or used or connected with home-built equipment then that warranty may be void.

First Published — January 1991
Revised Edition — August 1993
Reprinted — May 1995

British Library Cataloguing in Publication Data:

Kantaris, Noel
   A concise introduction to Microsoft works.
   1. Microcomputer systems. Software packages: Microsoft works
   I. Title II. Oliver, P.R.M.
   005.369

ISBN 0 85934 239 5

Printed and Bound in Great Britain by Cox & Wyman Ltd, Reading

ABOUT THIS BOOK

This Concise Introduction to Microsoft Works was written to help the beginner. The material in the book has been fully revised to cover Version 3.0 of the program and is presented on the "what you need to know first, appears first" basis. However the underlying structure is such that you don't have to start at the beginning and go right through to the end. The more experienced user can start from any section, as the sections have been designed to be self contained. The book does not, however, describe the workings of MS-DOS, or how to set up your computer hardware. If you need to know more about these, then may we suggest that you also refer to the book *A Concise User's Guide to MS-DOS 5* (BP318), which is also published by BERNARD BABANI (publishing) Ltd.

Microsoft Works is an integrated package containing four major types of applications; word processing, spreadsheet, database management and communications. The program is operated by selecting commands from menus, the keyboard, or Toolbars, or by writing special 'macros' to chain together menu commands. Each method of accessing the package is discussed separately, but the emphasis is mostly in the area of menu-driven command selection, rather than on macros. Using a mouse is not mandatory, but its use certainly increases productivity.

The power and versatility of Microsoft Works is evident in its integration which allows data from any module to be quickly and easily transferred into any of the other modules. The package is a powerful one, offering many commands, and functions, including a spell checker and a thesaurus. It is possible to use Lotus 1-2-3 (Version 1 and 2) files in Works, and a Works spreadsheet in 1-2-3 without any file conversions.

This book is intended as a supplement to the documentation that comes with the package. It provides the new user with a set of examples that aim to help with the learning of the most commonly used features of the package, and also provide the confidence needed to tackle some of the more advanced features of the package later. Emphasis has not been placed on the Communication tool, templates or the WorksWizards. It is felt that keen learners will benefit more from actually building their own applications.

TRADEMARKS

ABOUT THE AUTHORS

Noel Kantaris graduated in Electrical Engineering at Bristol University and after spending three years in the Electronics Industry in London, took up a Tutorship in Physics at the University of Queensland. Research interests in Ionospheric Physics, led to the degrees of M.E. in Electronics and Ph.D. in Physics. On return to the UK, he took up a Post-Doctoral Research Fellowship in Radio Physics at the University of Leicester, and in 1973 a Senior Lectureship in Engineering at Camborne School of Mines, Cornwall, where since 1978 he has also assumed the responsibility of Head of Computing.

Phil Oliver graduated in Mining Engineering at Camborne School of Mines in 1967 and since then has specialised in most aspects of surface mining technology, with a particular emphasis on computer related techniques. He has worked in Guyana, Canada, several Middle Eastern countries, South Africa and the United Kingdom, on such diverse projects as: The planning and management of bauxite, iron, gold and coal mines; rock excavation contracting in the U.K.; international mining equipment sales and technical back up; international mine consulting for a major mining house in South Africa. In 1988 he took up a Senior Lectureship at Camborne School of Mines in Surface Mining and Management.

If you would like to purchase a floppy disc containing all the files/programs which appear in this, or any other listed book(s) by the same author(s), then fill-in the form at the back of the book and send it to P. R. M. Oliver at the address stipulated.

ACKNOWLEDGEMENTS

We would like to thank the staff of Microsoft Corporation in the United Kingdom for providing the updated software on which this revision was based. We would also like to thank colleagues at both the Camborne School of Mines and Exeter University for the helpful tips and suggestions which assisted us in the writing of this book.

CONTENTS

1. PACKAGE OVERVIEW

Microsoft Works version 3.0 is an easy to use, integrated package. As with previous versions, it incorporates four full modules; word processing, spreadsheet with graphics, database, and communications, all of which are downward compatible with earlier versions. The package also comes with a calendar, its own front-end graphical interface, reminiscent of Microsoft Windows, with full documentation and with WorksWizards. These simplify several common procedures by stepping you through semi automated routines.

Installing Works

Microsoft Works can be installed on either an IBM PC or 100% compatible either on floppy discs, or on a hard disc. Obviously, you will get maximum advantage if you install it on hard disc. The installation of the program is made easy with the use of the **setup** program which allows you to specify the hardware peripherals and software components you will be using with Works by selecting items from various lists. The procedure takes about half an hour and you will need about 4.1 MB of available space on your hard disc. If necessary you could reduce this considerably in the future by dispensing with the tutorial and example files.

To use the **setup** program, insert the Works Setup disc in drive A:, and at the DOS prompt type

A:setup

You are given the options to:

Install Works 3.0 for the first time, or
Modify an existing working copy of Works 3.0

To select one of these, highlight your choice by using the up and down arrow keys and press the <Enter> key. To cancel the setup procedure at any time, hold the 'Ctrl' key down and press the 'X' key, (<Ctrl+X>).

The third screen gives you the choice of an automatic or manual installation. If you are at all in doubt here, choose the default and let Setup select the best options for your system. Select **Continue** to accept the destination directory C:\WORKS for the program, unless of course you prefer to install it elsewhere. The next screen offers you 5 choices depending on the type of display you have.

You are then given the option to install printer drivers. These are required by Works to control your printer. Follow the fairly detailed instructions given on the screen here as the procedure is not always intuitive! Unless your hardware setup is unusual, you should choose the LPT1 option for the printer port. If necessary, select as many printers as you need and then continue with the installation.

The next step involves you personalising your copy of the program by entering your name and, if relevant, your company name. When you are happy with your entries select **Continue**. The setup program then proceeds to create a subdirectory (if you chose to install on a hard disc) into which the various package files are copied. Finally the subdirectory \WORKS is added to the PATH statement in your AUTOEXEC.BAT file. Don't worry though, for safety the existing file is renamed AUTOEXEC.OLD, in case you need it again. All being well you should now have a full working version of Microsoft Works to get your teeth into.

Manual Options:

With a manual installation you have more control over the choice of hardware and you are asked whether you would like to set up Works to operate in 'Text mode' or 'Graphics mode'. Although in 'Text mode' the package works faster, 'Graphics mode' may be preferable since different character fonts and text enhancements (such as italics and underlining) can be displayed on the screen in the same way as they will appear when printed on paper. The choice is yours but if you have a VGA monitor, we suggest you choose the 'Graphics mode', otherwise choose the 'Text mode'. This choice is not critical, as you can always change it later, from within Works, by selecting the **Options, Works Settings** command.

Finally, you will be asked whether you want the 'Learning Works' tutorial to be copied on your hard disc. This choice depends on the available space on your disc. Without the tutorial, the program requires some 3 MB of disc space; with the tutorial a shade over 4 MB. If you don't copy the tutorial on the hard disc, you will not be able to activate it from within Works by selecting the **Help**, **Learning Works Tutorial** command.

Starting Works

To start Microsoft Works, assuming that you have followed all the manufacturer's instructions relating to the installation of the software, change to the subdirectory into which you have copied the package's files, say, **\WORKS** if you have installed onto the hard disc (by typing cd \WORKS at the DOS prompt), and type **works**. If you have installed the program on a floppy disc, you only need to type **works** at the A:\> DOS prompt.

As the \WORKS directory was placed on your path, you could in fact start the program from anywhere on your system by simply typing **works**. You would have the problem, though, of not being able to find your data files, unless you had launched Works from their directory.

You could simplify the hard disc operation by writing a batch file, call it **mw.bat**, to automatically change directory and execute the **works.exe** program file. The **mw.bat** batch file could contain the following commands:

```
@echo off
cls
c:
cd c:\works
works
cd c:\
```

If such a batch file has been written and placed in a directory on the system path, typing **mw** at the DOS prompt and pressing the <Enter> key, starts the program.

After the program file **works.exe** is loaded and executed, the main Works menu appears on the screen, first with the copyright declaration displayed and then with a list of starting options.

Starting Options:

These options allow you to jump quickly to part of the Works program. **Create a New File**, or **Open an Existing File**, place you straight away in the Works tool that uses the file type requested. **Use a WorksWizard** offers you a choice of semi-automated procedures to carry out. **Open the Calendar** lets you use the built in diary feature, **See an Introduction** gives you a quick tour of the Works program and **Help** describes the operation of the options box in more detail. We suggest you experiment with these later and at the moment simply press the <Esc> key, or select **Cancel**, to obtain the basic Works menu screen, shown below.

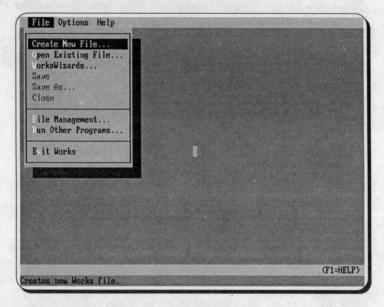

The main Works menu appears on the screen with the item 'File' in the main menu highlighted and with its pull-down sub-menu displayed underneath. The pull-down sub-menus associated with the other two items of the main menu can be seen by pressing the right arrow key. Pressing the <Esc> key clears the sub-menus.

The Main Menu:
As we have seen, each main menu option has associated with it a pull-down sub-menu. To activate the main menu, either press the <Alt> key, which causes the first letter of each item of the main menu to be displayed in bold, and the first item of the menu (in this case **File**) to be highlighted, then use the right and left arrow keys to highlight any of the items in the main menu, or use the mouse to point to an item. Pressing either the <Enter> key, or the left mouse button, reveals the pull-down sub-menu of the highlighted menu item.

Main menu options can also be activated directly by pressing the <Alt> key followed by the first letter of the required option. Thus pressing <Alt+O>, causes the pull-down sub-menu of the 'Options' to be displayed. You can use the up and down arrow keys to move the highlighted bar up and down a sub-menu, or the right and left arrow keys to move along the options of the main menu. As each option is highlighted, a short description of the function of the relevant option or command appears in the status line at the bottom of the screen. Pressing the <Enter> key selects the highlighted option or executes the highlighted command. Pressing the <Esc> key closes the menu system and returns you to the main menu. Selection of a sub-menu item can also be achieved by either typing the emboldened letter of the required command, or using the mouse to point to the required command and pressing the left mouse button.

If you use a mouse, you can select an item from the main menu by pointing to it and pressing the left mouse button; then, while the button is depressed, drag the mouse downwards on top of the revealed sub-menu which highlights each sub-menu item as you pass over it. Once the required item has been highlighted, release the mouse button to select it.

The Main Menu Options:
Each item of the main menu offers the following options:

File: Produces a pull-down menu, as shown, of mainly file related tasks, such as creating a new file, opening an existing file from disc and displaying it on screen, starting a WorksWizard, saving a file to disc, closing opened files, run file management commands or other programs and exiting Works.

Note that some sub-menu options, such as the **Save**, **Save As** and **Close** options, appear in fainter writing than, say, the **File Management** option. This means that you cannot access them. In this particular instance you cannot save work you have not created yet, or close a file that has not been opened.

Options: Defines the settings for Works, and activates the various accessories, such as the calculator, alarm, calendar and, if you have a modem connected to your system, a facility to dial a phone number.

Help: Activates the help window, displays the help contents, a search facility, a keyboard template, offers advice on how to use help or the Works package and gives access to the Works tutorial (if you have loaded the tutorial files on your hard disc).

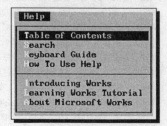

Help Screens:
Works has context-sensitive help screens which explain the use of the items in the various menus, or commands you are attempting to use. Thus, to obtain help information on the use of the options offered under **File**, as shown below, first choose

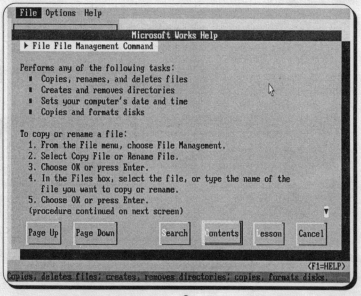

the **File** command, then use the down arrow key to highlight the desired task from the pull-down menu, and then press the **F1** function key.

Dialogue Boxes:
Three periods after a sub-menu option or command, means that a dialogue box will open when the option or command is selected. A dialogue box is used for the insertion of additional information, such as the name of a file under which to save your current work.

To illustrate this, select the **Options, Works Setting** command which will display the dialogue box shown below.

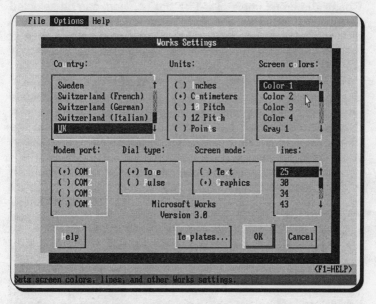

When a dialogue box opens, the <Tab> and <Shift+Tab> keys can be used to move the cursor from one field to another in a clockwise or anti-clockwise direction, respectively. Once in the selected field, the up and down arrow keys can be used to select different options. The <Enter> key is only used to indicate that the options within the various fields within the dialogue box are specified correctly.

Every dialogue box contains one field which is enclosed in double lines (**OK**, in the above example). This field indicates the

7

action that Works will take if the <Enter> key is pressed. These fields are referred to as command buttons. Pressing the <Esc> key, aborts the dialogue box and menu option and returns you to the main menu.

With a mouse, to select any item within any field, simply point to the desired item and click the left mouse button. To confirm your selections, click on the **OK** button. Clicking the **Cancel** button, aborts the dialogue box and menu option and returns you to the main menu.

There are five types of field boxes in a dialogue box; 'List', 'Option', 'Check', 'Text' and 'Command buttons'. Referring to the previous display on **Works Settings**, the first box under 'Country' is an example of a 'List' box. An item can be selected either by using the up and down arrow keys or by pointing and clicking at it with the mouse. If there are more options than fit the box, either use the down arrow key or click the down scroll arrow to see the next available option.

The second box under 'Units' in the **Works Settings** display, is an example of an 'Option' box. A dot enclosed in parentheses against an option signifies that the particular option is selected. Only one option can be selected at a time. To change the selected option, either press the emboldened letter of the option you want to select, or point to it with the mouse and click.

In a check box the options can either be 'on' (marked with an 'X' within square brackets) or 'off'. It is possible that you might want to use more than one option in a check box, for example you might want to enhance text by turning 'on' both bold and italic options from the 'Styles' check box.

A 'Text' box, is a box into which you can either type new information or change what is there by editing it. A blank text box is identified by a row of dots enclosed in square brackets. To change the selected option, either press the emboldened letter of the option you want to select, or point to it with the mouse and click.

You press a 'Command button' to execute a certain command, such as the **OK** button in the **Works Settings** display. Command buttons in Works are square and a preset button is shown edged with a double line. Most dialogue boxes have the three command buttons; **OK**, **Help** and **Cancel**. To select a command button, either use the <Tab> key to highlight it and press <Enter>, or point to it with the mouse and click.

The Works Screen:
It is perhaps worth spending some time looking at the various parts that make up the Works screen window. To illustrate our discussion, use the **File, Create New File** command if you are within Works. If not, start the program and select **Create a New File** from the opening options box. Both methods will open the following dialogue box.

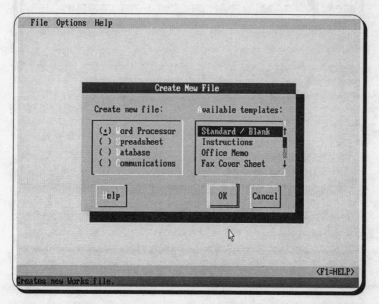

Choose the **Spreadsheet** option by pressing 'S', or by clicking it with your mouse and then selecting **OK**. Note that the screen window produced now displays a new list of menu names at the top, a Toolbar with a list of abbreviated command options below, a window title (SHEET1.WKS, in this case) below this, and an empty worksheet with numbered rows and lettered columns, as shown on the next page.

Although multiple worksheet, database and document files can be displayed simultaneously in their own windows, you can only enter data into the active window (highlighted at the top). Title bars of nonactive windows appear in a more darkened shade than that of the active one and have a single line on either side of the title, as opposed to the double line of the active window.

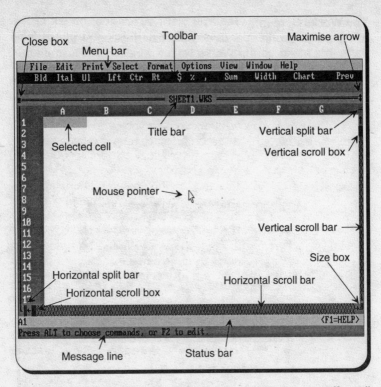

The Works screen is subdivided into several areas (for all Works modules - referred to as tools), which have the following function:

Area	*Function*
Menu bar	The bar displaying the various menus at the top of the screen which allow you to activate sub-menus. The names of the main menu commands might be different when using a different tool. To display a sub-menu, click on the name or press <Alt> followed by the emboldened letter.
Toolbar	When clicked on with the mouse provides short cuts for many of the more common commands in each tool.
Title bar	The bar which displays the window name (SHEET1.WKS, in our illustration).

Close box	The little black box at the top left of the screen which you click to close a window, or file.
Maximise arrow	The double headed arrow at the top right of the screen which you click to fill the screen with the active window.
Split bar	The horizontal or vertical double line situated above or adjacent to the up or left arrow of the scroll bars. You can split the screen horizontally or vertically by dragging a split bar.
Scroll bars	The area on the screen that contains arrowheads to which you can point and click to scroll the screen.
Scroll box	The horizontal or vertical solid box within the scroll bars which can be dragged to scroll by large amounts.
Size box	The box at the extreme right bottom of the screen where the two scroll bars meet. You can change the size of a window by dragging this box.
Status line	Displays the current program status and information regarding the present process.
Message line	Displays action to be taken or a short description of the highlighted command.

Manipulating Windows

Works allows the display of multiple sets of data within a given application tool, or several windows encompassing files from different application tools, each within its own window.

It is likely that at some stage you will want to manipulate these windows, by selecting which is to be the active window, moving them so that you can see all the relevant parts of an application, resizing them, or indeed closing unwanted windows once you have finished with them. A short discussion follows on how to manipulate windows so that you can get the best of what Works can provide.

In order to illustrate our discussion, use the **File, Create New File** command four successive times and choose, in turn, a different tool option from the four displayed in the dialogue box.

11

As each selection is made, a titled window is displayed with additional windows appearing on top of any existing windows, as shown below.

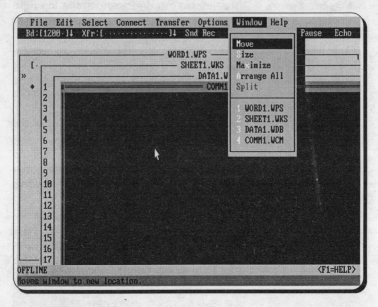

If you create a certain type of window file using the same tool more than once, this is reflected in the number appearing immediately after the default name of the particular window. You could save your work using different names than the default ones, (with each name no more than 8 characters long) but the three letter extension of the name of each tool is added by Works and remains the same, for each tool, as the ones displayed above. Note that the active window has a double line on either side of its title, while the nonactive ones have a single line.

The four application tools filename extensions are as follows:

Extension	Tool
WPS	Works Word Processor
WKS	Works Spreadsheet
WDB	Works Database
WCM	Works Communications.

12

Changing the Active Window:
You can select the active window amongst those displayed on the screen by pointing to any part of it, or its title, and clicking the mouse button, or by selecting the **Window** command of the main menu and selecting the appropriate number of the window you want to make the active one.

Closing a Window:
A window can be closed at any time once you have finished with it, provided it is the active window. To close the COMM1 window, make it the active window and either click on the little solid square at the upper left corner of the window, or use the **File, Close** command.
   If you have made any changes to a file in a window since the last time you saved it, Works will warn you with the appearance of a dialogue box giving you the option to save the file prior to closing it.

Moving a Window:
When you have multiple Works windows on the screen, you might want to move a particular window to a different part of the screen. Moving windows can be achieved with either the mouse or the keyboard.
   To move a window with the mouse, point to the title bar and drag it (press the left button and keep it pressed while moving the mouse) until the shadow border is where you would like it to be. Then release the mouse button to fix the window into its new position.
   To move a window with the keyboard, use the **Window, Move** command and the arrow keys to move the shadow border to the required position. Pressing <Enter>, fixes the window to its new position.

Sizing a Window:
You can change the size of an active window with either the mouse or the keyboard.
   To size with the mouse, move the window so that the 'size box' (at bottom right corner of the window) is visible, then drag the size box in the direction you want that corner to move. Continue dragging until the shadow border is the size you require, then release the mouse button.

13

To size with the keyboard, use the **Window, Size** command and press the appropriate arrow key for the direction you want that side or corner to move and continue to do so until the shadow border is the size you require, then press <Enter> to fix the new window size.

Maximising a Window:

To maximise a window, so that it fills the entire screen, either use the mouse to click on the maximise arrow (the double headed arrow on the top right corner of the window), or use the **Window, Maximize** command.

A maximised window can be returned to its original size and position on the screen by either clicking on the maximise arrow, or using the **Window, Maximize** command once more. The **Maximize** command is toggled on and off by the appearance of a dot against the option.

Splitting a Window:

The windows of two Works application tools can be split so that you can see different parts of your work side by side in the same window. You can split the word window horizontally and the spreadsheet window both horizontally and vertically.

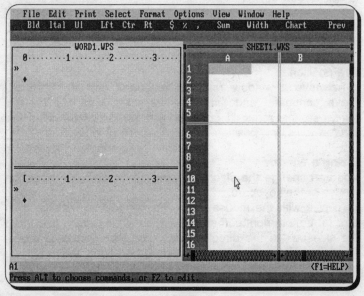

14

To split a window, either drag the split bar (the double lines to be found either below the maximise arrow or to the left of the horizontal scroll arrow) in the appropriate direction to the required position and release the mouse button, or use the **Window, Split** command, then the arrow keys to move the shadow split line to the required position and press <Enter>.

The previous figure shows the word processor window split into two areas and the spreadsheet window into four areas.

Viewing All Windows:
You can arrange to view all the windows currently on the screen by using the **Window, Arrange All** command. Works automatically arranges the windows on screen.

The following figure shows what will be displayed if you use this command with three windows open. The active window is always placed full height on the left of the screen.

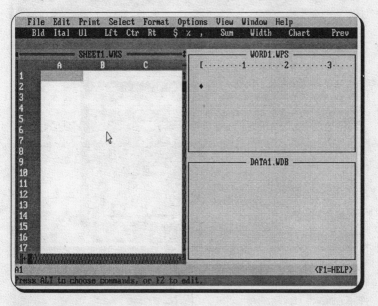

Managing Files
Works allows you to create, save, open, or generally operate on files, by using the **File** command from either the main menu of the package or from the menu of any of its tools. No matter from where the command is activated, the pull-down sub-menu

is the same, as was discussed under 'The Main Menu Options' section, at the beginning of this chapter. We have already discussed the use of the **File, Create New File** command, the first option of the sub-menu. Now we introduce the rest of these common commands.

Saving a File:
Once a document has been prepared, under any of the four tool applications, you can save it by using the **File, Save** command. The first time you use this command with, say, the word processor, Works asks you in a dialogue box for a filename to save under. With this tool, the default filename for the first opened window is WORD1.WPS, as shown below.

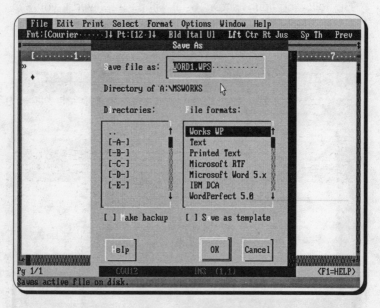

You can type a new name, say, MEMO (without the extension) and press <Enter> which causes the typed filename to become the new document title. Once a file has been saved, subsequent use of the **File, Save** command, saves the file automatically under the filename, directory and drive first used to save your work.

To change the drive or directory from its default, which might be C:\WORKS to, say, A:\MSWORKS, click at the [-A-] drive in the 'Directories' box and press the **OK** button. With the keyboard, press <Alt+i> (or press the <Tab> key once), to move into the **Directories** box, use the arrow keys to highlight the [-A-] drive, press <Enter> to select it and then highlight the required directory from the displayed list and press <Enter>.

If you want to save an already saved file under a different name, then use the **File, Save As** command. Works again offers you, in the same dialogue box, the original filename which you can change by typing a different name without an extension (the moment you start typing the new name, the default name vanishes from the display). On pressing <Enter>, the program adds automatically the appropriate extension for you.

The **File Formats** box allows you to save the file in any of the formats listed. You would select 'Wordperfect 5.1' for instance if you wanted to use the file later in that package.

Retrieving a File:
To retrieve an already saved document from disc, use the **File, Open Existing File** command. This will bring up the following dialogue box:

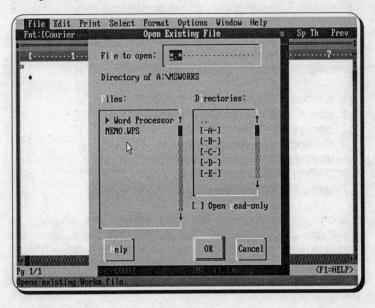

In this case the open directory is A:\MSWORKS and in the 'Files' box the appropriate file is displayed. To select the MEMO.WPS file, either click at its name, or press <Alt+F> (or press the <Tab> key once), to move into the **Files** box, highlight the required file and press <Enter>.

Using the Tutorials

Works comes with a set of comprehensive tutorials which can be accessed from within the package (provided you have installed them on the hard disc) by selecting the **Help, Learning Works Tutorial** command. Once you have "logged in" by entering your name, this brings up 6 topics on a newly designed graphics screen, namely:

1. Works Essentials
2. Word Processing
3. Spreadsheets & Charts
4. Databases & Reports
5. Communications
6. Using Tools Together

You can choose any of the options by pressing the emboldened letter in its title. Choosing, say, option 1, brings up a sub-menu which covers aspects on Works Essentials, as listed below. The approximate time required to go through each option is shown in brackets against the relevant option.

1. Keyboard and Mouse Introduction (3 mins)
2. How to Use this Course (8 mins)
3. Introducing Works (3 mins)
4. Starting with Works (15 mins)
5. Working with Files (25 mins)
6. Getting Assistance (12 mins)
7. Using Works with the Mouse (15 mins)

Although the contents of the early tutorials are simple, it is worth spending some time on them to, at least, learn the language and definitions associated with the various Works applications. However, if, say, you already know all there is to know about the keyboard and mouse, then start with the second or third option.

There is also an online tutorial help which can be accessed from within the package by pressing <Shift+F1>. Works will either display the lesson which relates to what you are currently doing, or if such lesson does not exist, it will display the Tutorial menu.

Exiting Works

Whenever you are ready to leave the Works package the procedure is the same whichever tool you are in. You simply use the **File**, **Exit Works** command. If all the open files have been saved, you will be returned immediately to DOS. If not, you will be given the option to save them, before they are lost forever.

2. THE WORKS WORD PROCESSOR

Works comes equipped with a word processor almost as powerful as most 'stand alone' versions. It has all the normal editing features, including the ability to insert, delete, erase, search for, replace, copy and move characters, lines and whole blocks of text. Works also allows you to enhance text and create bold, underlined, italic, strike-through, superscript, subscript and other specially formatted text.

Being an integrated package it is easy to embed part of a spreadsheet into a document, carry out a mail merge, or send a document to a distant computer using the communications functions.

Word Processor Basics

To access the word processor select **File, Create New File** from the opening menu bar, as described in the previous chapter. Then select **Word Processor** from the next list by either pressing the **W** key, or pressing <Enter>, as this is the highlighted option. A screen similar to that shown below will appear, with the file WORD1.WPS opened for you.

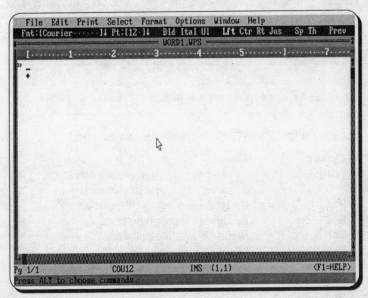

When you save your work later you should rename this, or else the file may be overwritten when WORD1.WPS is next opened automatically and saved again. If you open more than one new file, at the same time, they will be numbered Word1, Word2, and so on.

The Word Processor Screen:
The top line of this screen gives the menu bar, which with the word processor, accesses the following sub menus:

File	Edit	Print	Select	Format	Options	Window	Help

As described in the 'Package Overview' these are accessed either with your mouse, or by pressing the <Alt> key followed by the highlighted letter.

The Toolbar occupies the second line down. If you use a mouse you will find this a big time saver, once you get in the habit of using it. If you prefer, you can turn it off by activating the **Options**, **Show** command and clicking in the **Show Toolbar** check box. This is a toggle, when the 'X' shows the Toolbar will display, otherwise it will not. The only advantage to be gained by not showing it is you gain one screen line.

To use the Toolbar you simply click the mouse on one of the abbreviated options shown below, and the command selected will affect all text in the document that is highlighted.

Fnt:[Courier.....]® Pt:[12.]® Bld Ital Ul   Lft Ctr Rt Jus Sp Th Prev

The meanings of the Toolbar options are as follows:

Option	*Result*
Fnt:[..........]®	Choose font from available list. Clicking the arrow (®) will open the list of fonts.
Pt:[...]®	Choose from available point sizes.
Bld	Embolden highlighted text.
Ital	Make selected text italic
Ul	Underline text
Lft	Left align a paragraph
Ctr	Centre align a paragraph

22

Rt	Right align a paragraph
Jus	Justify a paragraph, between the left and right margins
Sp	Turn spell checker on
Th	Start thesaurus
Prev	Print preview the current page

The 'title bar' is the next line down. This shows the name of the opened document, and if this bar is dragged with the mouse the window can be moved around the screen.

Below the title bar is the ruler which appears as a scale across the screen. This shows the length of lines, the left and right margin positions and any tab or indent settings active in the paragraph the cursor is in. The ruler can be toggled on and off like the Toolbar, with the **Options, Show** command.

The bottom line of the screen is the message line which gives you useful information on the operation being carried out, or a description of the highlighted command. Above this is the status line which shows the current document page, the total number of pages, the font settings in operation, the cursor column and line position, any keys that are currently locked, and the reminder that pressing **F1** at any time will invoke the help function.

The scroll bars, boxes and arrows described in the Package Overview section also surround the work area which makes up the remainder of the screen.

Whenever a Works word processing file is opened three marks always appear in the top left corner of the screen working area:

»   is a page mark which identifies the beginning of a page.

_   the blinking underline is the cursor. Any text typed will be placed at this position.

♦   the end mark which identifies the end of a document. This mark cannot be erased from the screen. All text, etc., must be placed above it. The mark can be forced down the screen by pressing <Enter> when the cursor is above it, which inserts blank lines.

23

Entering Text:

Before going any further enter the following memo text, or something else if you prefer, to begin to get the feel of Works word processing.

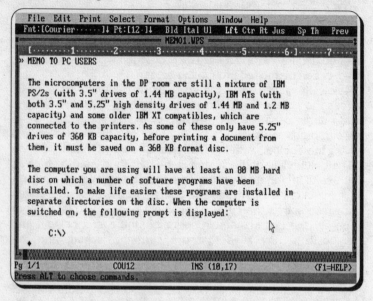

When a new file is opened it is ready for you to begin typing in text. Any time you want to force a new line, or paragraph, just press <Enter>. Otherwise the program will sort out line lengths automatically. This is known as word wrap. So, you can just carry on typing a complete paragraph without having to press any keys to move to a new line. If you make a mistake press <BkSp> enough times to erase the mistake and retype it.

Moving Around a Document:

You can move the cursor around a document with the normal direction keys, with the key combinations shown below, or with the **Select, Go To** command (or press **F5**). With the last command you can jump to various named 'bookmarks', or to different page numbers.

To move	Press
Left one character	←
Right one character	→

Up one line	↑
Down one line	↓
Left one word	Ctrl+←
Right one word	Ctrl+→
Up one paragraph	Ctrl+↑
Down one paragraph	Ctrl+↓
To beginning of line	Home
To end of line	End
To beginning of file	Ctrl+Home
To end of file	Ctrl+End
Up one window	Pg Up
Down one window	Pg Dn
To beginning of window	Ctrl+Pg Up
To end of window	Ctrl+Pg Dn

Now is a good time to save the document, as described in the previous chapter, press **File, Save As** and type a new drive, path and filename. For example, change to **A:\MEMO1** to save to a floppy disk in the A: drive. The program will add the WPS extension for you.

Document Editing

It will not be long when using the word processor before you will need to edit your screen document. This could be to delete unwanted words, correct a mistake or to add extra text in the document. All these operations are very easy to carry out.

For small deletions, such as letters or words, the easiest method is using the <Del> or <BkSp> keys. With the <Del> key, position the cursor on the first letter to delete and press <Del>; the letter is deleted and the following text moves one space to the left.

With the <BkSp> key, position the cursor immediately to the right of the character to be deleted and press <BkSp>; the cursor moves one space to the left pulling the rest of the line with it and overwriting the character to be deleted.

Note that the difference between the two is that with <Del> the cursor does not move at all.

Word processing is usually carried out in the insert mode. Any characters typed will be inserted at the cursor location and the following text will be pushed to the right, and down, to make room. When in this mode the letters 'INS' will show in the middle of the status line. Pressing <Ins> then will change you to overstrike mode and the letters 'OVR' will appear. In this mode any text you type will over-write existing text.

To insert blank lines in your text, make sure you are in Insert mode, place the cursor at the beginning of the line where the blank is needed and press <Enter>. The cursor line will move down leaving a blank line. To remove the blank line position the cursor at its left end and press <Del>.

When larger scale editing is needed, such as using the copy, move and erase operations, the text to be altered must be 'selected', or 'highlighted', before the operation can be carried out. These functions are then available when the **Edit** sub-menu is activated, or the Toolbar options used.

Selecting Text:
The procedure in Works, before any operation such as formatting or editing can be carried out on text, is first to select the text to be altered. Selected text is highlighted on the screen. This can be carried out in several ways.

Using the keyboard, position the cursor on the first character to be selected and either:

a.   Hold down the <Shift> key while using the direction keys to highlight the required text, then release the <Shift> key, or:

b.   Press the **F8** key and use the direction keys to highlight the required text, or:

c.   Press **F8** TWO times to select a WORD
Press **F8** THREE times to select a SENTENCE
Press **F8** FOUR times to select a PARAGRAPH
Press **F8** FIVE times to select whole DOCUMENT.

With the mouse:

a.   Left click at the beginning of the block and drag the cursor across the block so that the desired text is highlighted, then release the mouse button.

b.   With the cursor in a word press the right mouse button to select that word.

c.   Position the cursor in the left window margin and:
Click the left button to select the current LINE
Click the right button to select the current PARAGRAPH
Click both buttons to select the entire DOCUMENT.

When using the **F8** key method, the message 'EXT' is displayed on the status line to indicate that extended highlighting of text is taking place. This mode can be cancelled by pressing <Esc>, or the selection can be collapsed one level by pressing <Shift+F8>.

Try out all these methods and find which you are most comfortable with.

Copying Blocks of Text:
Once text has been selected it can be copied to another location in your present document, to another Works document (as long as it is open), or even to another Works tool. As with most of the editing and formatting operations there are two ways of doing this. The first is by using the **Edit, Copy** command sequence from the menu, moving the cursor to the start of where you want the copied text, and pressing <Enter>. The other method uses the quick key combination <Shift+F3>, once the text to be copied has been selected, which does not require the menu bar to be activated. As you get used to the Works package you will be able to save a lot of time by using quick key combinations.

To copy the same text again to another location in the document, move the cursor to the new location and press <Shift+F7>. This operation is often called 'pasting' text, reminiscent of the old days of scissors and a glue pot!

Quick Key Combinations:
The following quick key combinations can be used in all the Works tools:

Editing
Move selection	F3
Copy selection	Shift+F3
Repeat search	F7
Repeat copy	Shift+F7
Insert date	Ctrl+;
Insert time	Ctrl+:

Combinations for use in the word processor only:
General Editing
Undo last command	Alt+BkSp
Delete selection	Del

Paragraph mark	Enter
Manual page break	Ctrl+Enter
Paginate now	F9
End of line mark	Shift+Enter
Optional hyphen	Ctrl+- (hyphen)
Non-breaking hyphen	Ctrl+_ (underline)
Non-breaking space	Ctrl+Shift+Spacebar
Print page number	Ctrl+P
Print filename	Ctrl+F
Print date	Ctrl+D
Print time	Ctrl+T

Character Styles

Bold	Ctrl+B
Italic	Ctrl+I
Strikethrough	Ctrl+S
Underline	Ctrl+U
Subscript	Ctrl+=
Superscript	Ctrl++
Plain text	Ctrl+Spacebar

The majority of the above need a block to be selected before they can be used.

Paragraph Formats

Normal paragraph	Ctrl+X
Centre	Ctrl+C
Justify	Ctrl+J
Left-align	Ctrl+L
Right-align	Ctrl+R
Hanging indent	Ctrl+H
Undo hanging indent	Ctrl+G
Nested indent	Ctrl+N
Undo nested indent	Ctrl+M
Single space	Ctrl+1
1½ space	Ctrl+5
Double space	Ctrl+2
One line before paragraph	Ctrl+O
No lines before paragraph	Ctrl+E

The above key combinations work on the paragraph holding the cursor, or on all the paragraphs currently selected.

Moving Blocks of Text:
Selected text can be moved to any location on the same document. Press either **Edit, Move,** (or **F3**), move the cursor to the required new location and press either <Enter> or use the **Edit, Move** command again. The moved text will be placed at the cursor location and will force any existing text to make room for it. This operation can be cancelled before the final key command by simply pressing <Esc>.

Replacing Blocks of Text:
One block of text can be 'replaced' by another using either the move or copy commands. Obviously if move is used the text at the original location will be lost, but not if the copy command is used. The process is the same as an ordinary copy or move, except that the block of text to be replaced must be selected before the final **Edit, Move** or **Edit, Copy** commands are made.

Deleting Blocks of Text:
When text is deleted it is removed from the document. With Works any selected text can be deleted by pressing **Edit, Delete,** or by simply pressing the <Del> key.

The UNDO Command:
As text is lost with the delete command you should use it with caution, but if you do make a mistake all is not lost as long as you act immediately. The **Edit, Undo** command reverses your most recent editing or formatting command, so you need to use it before carrying out any further operations. The quick key sequence for this command is <Alt+BkSp>.

Page Breaks:
The program automatically inserts a page break in a document when a page of typed text is full. The page break symbol (») tells the printer where to end one page and start printing another. There will be places in most multi-page documents where you will want to force a new page to improve the layout. This is done by inserting a manual page break by pressing **Print, Insert Page Break,** or just using the key combination <Ctrl+Enter>. Works readjusts all the non-manual page breaks for the remainder of the document.

To demonstrate this, retrieve the document previously saved as MEMO1.WPS. Note there is a page marker on the left hand side of line 1, in the margin next to the title line. Press <Ctrl+End> to place the cursor at the end of the document and just above the end of file marker. If you try to move down further, your computer will beep at you. Insert a page break as described above (**Print, Insert Page Break**). Your cursor should now be at the start of Page 2, with a line of dots indicating where the manual break was placed, as shown below.

Now press <Enter> repeatedly (or type lots of text) until the status line indicates 'Pg 3/3'. This is just a quick way of adding another page, albeit an empty one, to the document. Move the cursor up to the page break which was automatically inserted between pages 2 and 3. There is no line of dots. A manual page break can be deleted, but an automatic one cannot, so they appear differently on the screen.

Frustratingly, Works can take several seconds to sort out its automatic page breaks, especially with a long document, and it can fall behind you. If this becomes a problem simply press the **F9** key to force an immediate repagination of the document.

Document Navigation:
Now we have several 'pages' in a document it is a good time to explore some methods of navigating large documents. There are two main methods of jumping to specific document locations. Both use the **Select, Go to** command, or **F5** for short. This brings up the dialogue box shown on the next page.

Type **3** in the **Go to** text box, press <Enter> and your screen should jump straight to the top of page 3 in the document. This is a quick way of moving to the top of any page.

The other method uses the same box but uses 'bookmarks' which you place at strategic locations in your document. To place a bookmark in a document locate the cursor where you want the mark. In our example set the cursor at the beginning of the second paragraph of text, and press **Edit, Bookmark**

<u>Name.</u> Type **Two** in the empty dialogue box, as shown below and then press <Alt+C> to create the bookmark.

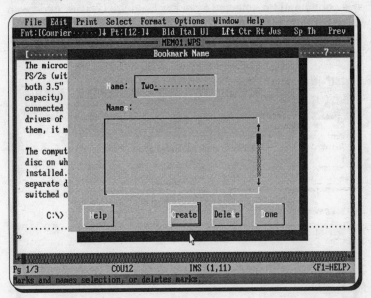

Your bookmark, although not visible on the screen, should still have been created. To test it, move to the end of the document with the <Ctrl+End> keys and press **F5**. 'Two' should now appear in the box under <u>Names.</u> Highlight this in the list, press <Enter>, and the cursor should jump to the second paragraph where the bookmark was placed. In a long document placing bookmarks at the start of each section makes it easy to find your way around.

Character Enhancement

Another simplistic example will explain the principles of text enhancement. With Works it is usually easier to type your text in first and worry about the document layout later on. Create a new word processing file and type in the letter text shown on the next page.

The date formula *date* on line 5 will give the current date when the letter is printed, and is generated with the quick key combination <Ctrl+D>. Alternatively, the current date could have been placed straight into the letter with the <Ctrl+;> keys.

If you cannot remember these key combinations don't worry, there is always another way of carrying out their functions. All of the above can be selected from the dialogue box activated with the **Edit**, **Insert Special Character** command. When you have finished, save the document using the **File, Save As** command, calling it LETTER1.

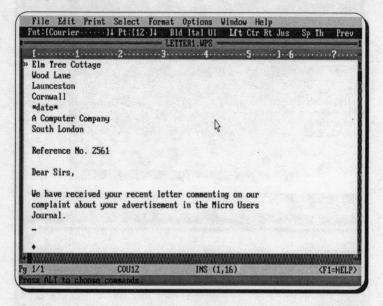

```
   File  Edit  Print  Select  Format  Options  Window  Help
  Fnt:[Courier······]↓ Pt:[12·]↓   Bld Ital Ul   Lft Ctr Rt Jus   Sp Th   Prev
 ═══════════════════════════ LETTER1.WPS ═══════════════════════════
  [·······1········2·······3········4·······5···]·6·······7····
 » Elm Tree Cottage
   Wood Lane
   Launceston
   Cornwall
   *date*
   A Computer Company
   South London                          ⤧

   Reference No. 2561

   Dear Sirs,

   We have received your recent letter commenting on our
   complaint about your advertisement in the Micro Users
   Journal.
   ▬

 ♦
 ─────────────────────────────────────────────────────────────
 Pg 1/1              COU12            INS (1,16)         <F1=HELP>
 Press ALT to choose commands.
```

To improve the layout of the letter we will use some of the commands in the **Format** sub-menu and also some of the Toolbar options.

First select the top five lines containing the address and date (the easiest way of doing this is to click the mouse alongside line one, in the left margin, and drag it down to line 5) and then press **Format, Right.** The whole block should now be 'right justified'. By default paragraphs are 'left justified'. While the block is still highlighted click the mouse on the **Lft** option of the Toolbar. Now press the <Ctrl+R> keys and you should be back with a right justified address.

Then select the Ref.... line of text and press **Format, Center** (or the quick keys <Ctrl+C>, or the **Ctr** Toolbar option) to centre the line between the left and right margins. While the selection highlight is still active press **Format, Underline** (or <Ctrl+U>, or

UI on the Toolbar) to underline the reference. By now you have probably accepted that the Toolbar is by far the most convenient way of carrying out these enhancement functions. If you repeat the Toolbar click while the highlight is still active the feature is turned off again. They act as toggle functions.

Next, select the words 'recent letter' and press <Ctrl+B>, or Toolbar **Bld**, to embolden them. Finally, select the section 'Micro Users Journal' and change them to italics by pressing **Format, Italic,** or <Ctrl+I>, orToolbar **Ital**.

The letter now looks very different and should be similar to LETTER2.WPS shown below.

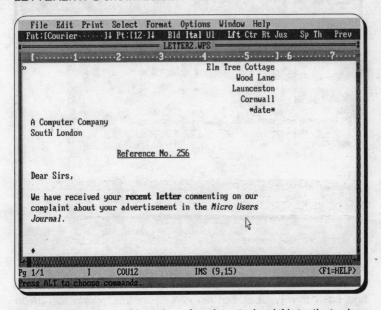

What a difference with only a few keystrokes! Note that when the cursor is in text that has been enhanced, a code appears on the screen status bar. The "I" above means the cursor is in an italicised area. A "U" shows for underlined text and a "B" when it is emboldened. These status indicators are useful when you are working in Text mode and the enhancements are not obvious from the screen text colours.

Fonts:

A font is a typeface with a specific design. In Works 3.0 you can print text in any fonts, or colours, which are supported by your printer, but the fonts do not appear any different on the normal editing screen.

To change the font, size, colour or enhancements of specific text in a document, first select the text. Choose the **Forma_t, _Font & Style** command, and make selections in the respective boxes, as shown below.

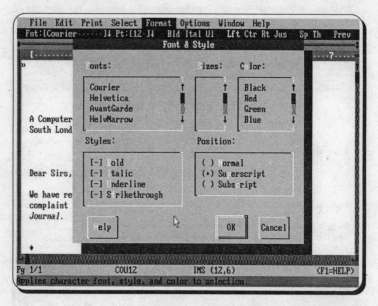

You can also, of course, change the font and size of selected text from the Toolbar **Fnt** and **Pt** options. Clicking the arrow alongside each opens up a drop-down menu of available options.

Works measures font sizes in points, where one point is 1/72nd of an inch. You will need to study your printer manual and experiment with these commands to make the most of this Works facility.

One thing to remember is that a printed page usually looks better if you use different fonts sparingly.

3. ADVANCED WP FEATURES

Paragraph Formatting

Works defines a paragraph, as any text which is followed by a paragraph mark (which appears as a '¶' character on the screen, but only when switched on). So single line titles, as well as long typed text, can form paragraphs. Paragraph markers are not normally shown in Works, but toggling the **Options, Show**, **Show All Characters** command, will toggle them on and off. A paragraph marker is placed in a document every time <Enter> is pressed. All paragraph formatting, such as alignment, justification, centring, indenting and line spacing, is stored in the marker for the particular paragraph. If this marker is deleted, or moved, the formatting will be deleted or moved with it.

Indenting Text:

Most documents with lists, or numbered sections, will require some form of paragraph indenting. An indent is the space between the margin and the edge of the text in the paragraph. This can be on the left or right side of the page.

Retrieve the file MEMO1.WPS and type '1. ' and '2. ' before the first words of the two main text paragraphs. Select the two paragraphs and press **Format, Indents & Spacing** to bring up the dialogue box shown on the next page.

Most of the paragraph formatting operations can either be carried out from the Toolbar, or from this box. The alignment box offers:

Left	Smooth left edge, jagged right
Center	Text centred on line
Right	Smooth right edge, jagged left
Justified	Smooth left and right edges

To create left or right indents for the whole paragraph, type the amount of indent in the respective space, in inches. If only the first line is to be indented, type the amount needed in the **1st line indent** space.

To keep a paragraph intact on one page check the **Don't break this paragraph** box. Select **Keep this paragraph with next** to anchor paragraph text together on a page.

Hanging Indents:

The dialogue box below is set up to produce hanging indents, so that the paragraph numbers show up clearly at the left of the paragraphs.

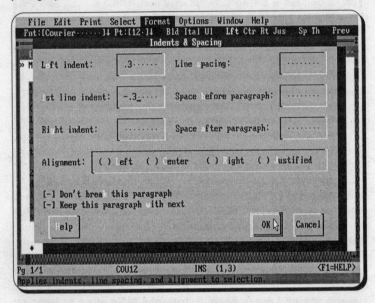

To do this you should type the same value in the **1st line indent** space - with a negative sign in front - as that typed in the **Left indent** space. When you have finished, and saved the document as MEMO2.WPS, your screen should look the same as that in the diagram on the next page.

Hanging indents can also be created with the quick key combination <Ctrl+H>. If no dialogue box has previously been completed, the indents are set to the next tab stop. <Ctrl+G> will remove the hanging indent.

Two fascinating key combinations to play with are those to produce and remove nested indents - <Ctrl+N> and <Ctrl+M>. These move the whole paragraph holding the cursor, to the next tab stop, to the right or left respectively, and maintain any hanging indents. With the careful use of these keys, lists and outlines are easy and fun to prepare.

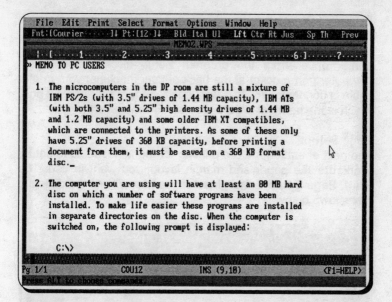

```
 File  Edit  Print  Select  Format  Options  Window  Help
Fnt:[Courier······]↓ Pt:[12·]↓   Bld Ital Ul   Lft Ctr Rt Jus   Sp Th   Prev
                          MEMO2.WPS
 ┆·[·····1·······2·······3·······4·······5·······6·]·····?····
» MEMO TO PC USERS

  1. The microcomputers in the DP room are still a mixture of
     IBM PS/2s (with 3.5" drives of 1.44 MB capacity), IBM ATs
     (with both 3.5" and 5.25" high density drives of 1.44 MB
     and 1.2 MB capacity) and some older IBM XT compatibles,
     which are connected to the printers. As some of these only
     have 5.25" drives of 360 KB capacity, before printing a
     document from them, it must be saved on a 360 KB format
     disc._

  2. The computer you are using will have at least an 80 MB hard
     disc on which a number of software programs have been
     installed. To make life easier these programs are installed
     in separate directories on the disc. When the computer is
     switched on, the following prompt is displayed:

     C:\>

Pg 1/1              COU12              INS (9,18)              <F1=HELP>
Press ALT to choose commands.
```

Paragraph Borders:

Unfortunately the Works package does not have a line drawing capability as such, but it is possible to place different types of lines at the top, bottom, sides, or all round individual paragraphs, with the **Format, Borders** command.

In the Border box, this command produces, turn on the border you want, in the Line style box select either **Normal**, **Bold** or **Double**, select a **Color** (in spite of the American spelling) and then press <Enter>. To remove borders you must cancel the selections made in these boxes.

Printing Documents

When Microsoft Works was first installed on your computer the printers you intend to use should have been selected, and their drivers copied to the program directory. Before printing for the first time, it is essential to ensure that your printer is properly installed.

Printer Setup:

This is done by checking the dialogue box which appears by choosing the **Print, Printer Setup** command. Make sure that the correct printer and model are listed. If not, click the **Change**

Printer & Option command button to access the list of installed printers. If your printer is not on this either, select the nearest printer on the list, or select **Install New** to load up the correct printer driver from the program Setup discs. Select which computer port (socket at the back of your machine) your printer cable is connected to. This will usually be **LPT1** for parallel port, which is the norm, or **COM1** for a serial connection.

Page Setup:

The next operation, before printing for the first time, is to set up Works for the paper and margin layout you want to use. The **Print, Page Setup & Margins** command produces the dialogue box shown below.

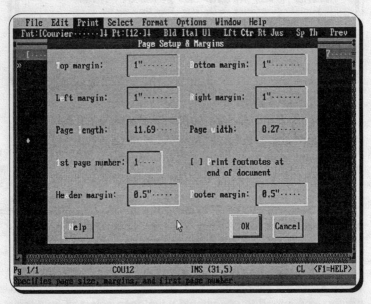

The above setup is for A4 paper size (11.69" x 8.27"). If you want to use a different size paper just type in new dimensions for **Page length** and **Page width.** The default is portrait mode. If you require landscape mode, and your printer supports it, simply swap the length and width dimensions around.

The **Top, Bottom, Left** and **Right** margins are the non-print areas required on each edge of the paper. The **Header** margin is that required between the top of the page and the header line. The **Footer** margin is that between the bottom of the page and the footer line.

The **1st page number** will normally be '1' unless you break up a piece of work into parts, or chapters, and have each one in a separate document file. This facility then allows you to adjust the page numbering of each.

Inserting a Graphic:

Microsoft Works 3.0 has the ability to include graphics and illustrations in a document. You cannot actually see them on the editing screen, but you can in the print preview described next.

Nine simple graphics are included with the package and you can import other files with the following filename extensions - .PCX, .TIF and .EPS. We would not recommend you being too ambitious here though. The following example is set up to show how to import a graphic image.

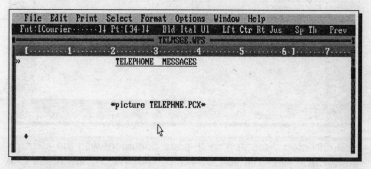

The title line was centred and the text set to 34 Pts on the Toolbar. Two empty lines were placed by pressing the <Enter> key twice and the **Edit**, **Insert Picture** command was used to select the graphics file TELEPHNE.PCX from the list of those in the Works program directory. Note that a code is inserted and centred on the line in the document that was holding the cursor.

Print Preview:

Works gives you an easy way of checking what your printer will produce with the **Print, Preview** command. After completing the dialogue box, if you want to print one copy of, or preview, the whole of a document, just press <Enter>.

Printing to a file produces a file with not only the text, but all the printer commands as well. Such a file can be printed from

DOS with the Copy command, for example, on a different computer without using the Works program at all.

From the dialogue box choose **Preview** to see a screen view of what the printed page should look like, similar to that shown below.

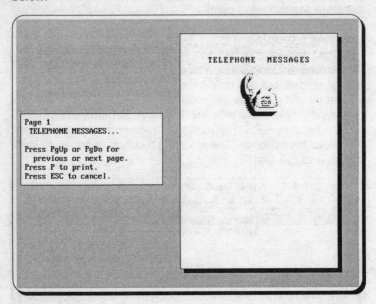

You can step through a multi-page document with the <PgUp> and <PgDn> keys. If you are happy with the preview press **P** to print the selected pages, otherwise press <Esc> to exit Preview.

Text Enhancement

Tab Settings:
Works defaults to left aligned tabs every half inch across the page. For most purposes these will be adequate, but if you need to generate lists, or tables, the custom tab facility should prove useful. There are four types of custom tab stops:

Left	Text aligns to the right of tab
Right	Text aligns to the left of tab
Center	Text centres on tab stop
Decimal	Text aligns at a decimal point

Default tab settings do not show on the ruler at the top of the screen, but custom tabs do. All default tabs to the left of a new custom tab are removed automatically.

You can also select one of four types of leader characters to fill the space to the tab spot. This is useful when preparing contents pages.

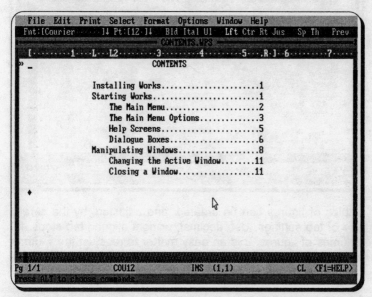

The above example shows part of a contents page which has two **Left** aligned tabs for the subjects, and a **Right** tab with a dot leader for the page numbers. The leader symbol can be seen on the ruler immediately in front of the "R".

To set custom tab stops, select the required paragraph, or the whole document, and choose **Format, Tabs**. A dialogue box like the one shown on the next page will open.

Use the mouse, or press <Ctrl+←> or <Ctrl+→>, to move the cursor to the correct position on the ruler. Select the options needed from the Alignment and Leader boxes and choose **Insert** to place the tab on the ruler. This operation can be repeated for as many tabs as are required. Use the **Delete**, or **Delete all** buttons to remove one tab, or all the tabs, from the ruler.

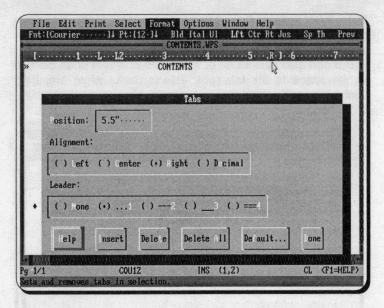

CONTENTS

Tabs

Position: | 5.5"······ |

Alignment:

( ) Left ( ) Center (•) Right ( ) Decimal

Leader:

( ) None (•) ...1 ( ) ─2 ( ) __3 ( ) ==4

[Help] [Insert] [Delete] [Delete All] [Default...] [Done]

Pg 1/1   COU12   INS (1,2)   CL <F1=HELP>
Sets and removes tabs in selection.

Tables of figures can be created, and adjusted, by the careful use of tab settings. Use decimal, or right aligned tab stops, for columns of figures. It is an easy matter to readjust the width of columns by resetting the tabs, even after the table has been created.

Headers and Footers:

In a printed document a header is text that appears at the top of each page of the document, whilst a footer appears at the bottom. These can be used to add page numbers, titles, dates and times to your documents. In the word processor it is possible to add two kinds of headers and footers - both paragraph and standard types.

Standard ones are typed in a dialogue box, and alignment characters are required to force their printed positions. Paragraph headers and footers have a special paragraph for each, placed at the top of the document, and text can be added and formatted as in the rest of the document.

Header and footer paragraphs are shown in the next example. These were added to the file MEMO2.WPS by choosing the **Print, Headers & Footers** command, turning on the **Use Header & Footer Paragraphs** check box, and pressing <Enter>.

Note that the program turns on the separate header and footer paragraphs, and also places an automatic page number placeholder in the centre of the footer line. (Page - *Page*). This will print the correct page number on every page. If page numbering is not required this can be deleted, or the code can be moved to another location on the header or footer lines.

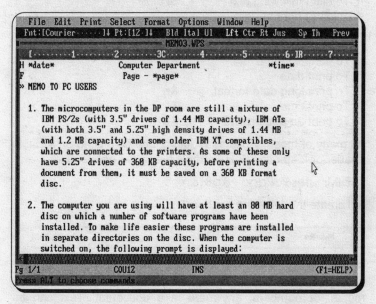

Move the cursor to the start of the header paragraph and add the date special command <Ctrl+D>. This adds *Date* to the screen, but will print the current date on paper. Press <Tab> and the cursor is automatically centred on the line. Add a title and press <Tab> three times to bring the cursor to the right hand side of the page. Add the time special command <Ctrl+T>, and save as MEMO3.

Your screen should now look like that shown above. If you want, you can add enhancements, or change the fonts of the header and footer text.

In the Spreadsheet or Database Works tools only standard headers and footers can be used. As these can also be used in the Word processor, we will describe them here. Choose **Print**,

Headers & Footers, as before, and type the required text in the two boxes. You can align parts of a standard header or footer, and include other items automatically, by typing any of the special codes from the following list in with the text. Note that, unless you change the alignment, standard headers and footers are automatically centred.

Operation	*Special Code*
To align following text at left or right margin	&l or &r
To centre the following text	&c
To print page number	&p
To print filename	&f
To print date	&d
To print long date format	&n
To print time	&t
To print an ampersand	&&

As many of these codes as required, can be placed on a single header or footer line. For example typing the header line:

&lMinutes&cPage - &p&r&n

will create the following header:

Minutes	Page - 6	June 20, 1993

Footnotes:
A useful feature added to Works is the ability to place reference marks, or numbers, anywhere in a document. Text can be 'attached' to each reference, which will automatically be printed at the end of the document. This operation is carried out with the **Edit, Footnote** command.

Footnotes are automatically numbered, and renumbered if edited, but you can also specify other reference marks (such as * or $, for example).

To create a footnote, move the cursor to the position in the document where the reference mark is needed, choose **Edit, Footnote,** alter the dialogue box if you want to force a mark instead of a numbered reference, and press <Enter>. If **Numbered** is selected in the box, the next consecutive footnote number is placed at the cursor and the footnote pane is opened in the bottom half of the screen. Type the reference text in this

44

pane, and format, or enhance it, if required. You can move the cursor back to the document either with the mouse, or by pressing **F6**.

Once placed there, footnote reference marks are always shown in the document. The footnote text itself can be shown, or switched off, by toggling the **Options**, **Show**, **Show Footnotes** command. In the example below this option has been selected.

Footnote text can be edited, the same as any other text, once the footnote pane is opened. Reference marks can also be moved, copied or deleted, and Works will look after the positioning of the attached text.

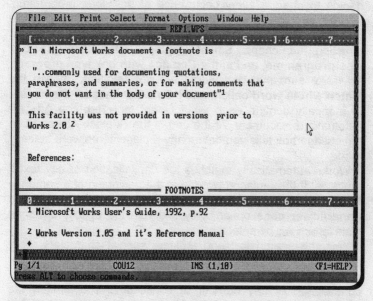

By default with Works 3.0 footnotes are printed at the bottom of each page, not at the end of the document as they were in the previous version. If you want them printed at the document end, check the **Print footnotes at end of document** box produced by the **Print**, **Page Setup & Margins** command.

In either case, final printed presentation is improved if you place blank lines at the end of the document text. Without these the footnote text will be printed immediately under the last page or document line. Any reference heading required should be placed after these lines, at the end of the document. The footnotes themselves look better, when printed, if a blank line is placed between each one, in the footnote pane, as shown on the previous page.

Searching for and Replacing Text:
Works allows you to search for specifically selected text, or character combinations. In the search mode it will highlight each occurrence in turn so that you can carry out some action on it, such as change its font or appearance. In the replace mode you specify what replacement is to be automatically carried out. For example, in a long book chapter you may decide to change every occurrence of the word 'programme' with the word 'program'. This is very easy to do. First go to the beginning of the file, as search only operates in a forward direction, then choose **Select, Replace.** In the **Search for** box type **programme**, and in the **Replace with** box type **program**. To make sure that part words are not selected, choose the **Match whole word** option, and then either choose <**Replace**>, to manually confirm each replacement, or <**Replace All**> for automatic replacement. At the end of the Replace All operation a message box tells you how many replacements were actually made.

Works automatically matches the capitalisation of any text it replaces. If the replaced word is at the beginning of a sentence it will capitalise the first letter. If you select the **Match upper/lower case** option, only text with the exactly specified case letters will be selected.

You can search for, and replace, special characters, or a combination of text and special characters (for example, tab or paragraph marks, or white space). White space is a combination of any number of consecutive spaces and tab marks. A very useful example of this is when you have imported columnar data from another file, and the columns are separated with spaces; you can search for white space, and replace it with a tab, to realign the columns.

Another example would be searching for a word, which occurs at the beginning of a paragraph, or after a tab.

The list on the next page gives the key combinations of special characters to type into search and replace boxes.

To type the caret (^) character, press **Shift+6.**

To search for or replace	*Type*
Tab mark	^t
Paragraph mark	^p
End-of-line mark	^n
Manual page break mark	^d
Non-breaking space	^s
Optional hyphen	^-
Non-breaking hyphen	^~
Caret (^)	^^
Question mark (?)	^?
Any ASCII character (#=ASCII No)	^#
White space	^w
Any character (wild card)	?

Using the Spell Checker:
If you have a problem with spelling, the spell checker in Works will be a popular part of the package! It will search for wrongly spelled words, words with incorrect capitalisation, incorrect hyphenation, and repeated words, such as 'if if'. It has a built in dictionary of some 120,000 words, and you can add other words that you may need to check for in the future.

To check the spelling of a whole document, move the cursor to the beginning with <Ctrl+Home>. Alternatively, you can select the text you want checked. In either case, invoke the checker by choosing **Options, Check Spelling.** When a word that is not recognised is found, a box appears as shown in the example on the next page. A problem message will appear in the top left corner of the box, the suspect word will be highlighted in the document, and will also be placed in the **Replace with** box.

You have several options now:

a.   To leave the word unchanged choose **Ignore**

b.   To change the word, edit, or retype it, in the box, and choose **Change,** or **Change All** to change all instances of that word.

c.   Choose **Suggest,** to view a list of proposed spellings from the dictionary, select one and choose **Change.**

d.   To add an edited word to the dictionary choose **Add.**

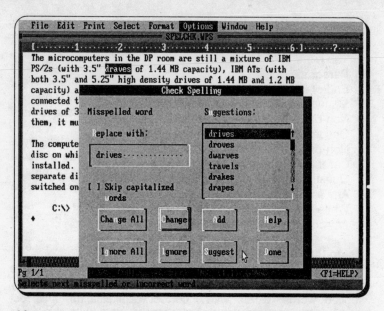

After you have chosen **Add, Ignore** or **Change,** the program continues searching the rest of the document. To leave the checker at any time simply choose **Done,** or press <Esc>.

Using the Thesaurus:

To help you with composing your documents Works has a built in thesaurus. With this you should be able to find a synonym, or word with a similar meaning, for most words, as shown below.

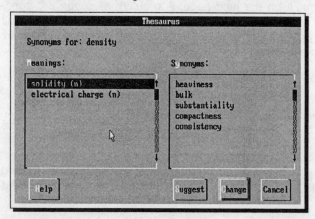

First select the word you want to change, and choose **Options, Thesaurus.** The dialogue box with two main sections comes onto the screen, as shown on the previous page.

In the **Meanings** box, on the left, are suggestions of the main meanings of the selected word. Depending on the context in the document, you need to select one of these meanings, and then look in the **Synonyms** box for a list of possible replacement words.

In the example previously given 'density' was the word highlighted in the document. The noun 'solidity' was selected from the **Meanings** list and pressing the **Suggest** command button produced the five synonyms shown. Sometimes the logic of the choices has to make you smile.

If you select one of the synonyms and press **Suggest** you should get more suggestions.

To replace the original word highlighted in your document, select the best alternative and choose **Change.**

Word Count:
Version 3.0 of Works now includes the facility to count the words in a document, or block of selected text. This can be useful if you are working on an assignment that requires a specific number of words.

Select the text to be counted and use the **Options**, **Word Count** command. If no text is selected the whole document will be counted. Works considers a word to be any text between two space characters.

4. THE WORKS SPREADSHEET

When you first enter the Works spreadsheet, the program sets up a huge electronic page, or worksheet, in your computer's memory, many times larger than the small part shown on the screen. Individual cells are identified by column and row location (in that order), with the present size extending to 256 columns by a massive 16,384 rows. The columns are labelled from A to Z, followed by AA to AZ, BA to BZ, and so on, to IV, while the rows are numbered from 1 to 16,384.

Using the **File, Create New File** command and selecting the **Spreadsheet** option from the dialogue box, displays:

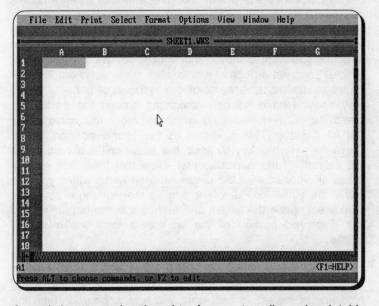

A worksheet can be thought of as a two-dimensional table made up of rows and columns. The point where a row and column intersect is called a cell, while the reference points of a cell are known as the cell address. The active cell (A1 when you first enter the program) is highlighted.

51

Worksheet Navigation

Navigation around the worksheet is achieved by the use of the four arrow keys. Each time one of these keys is pressed, the active cell moves one position right, down, left or up, depending on which arrow key was pressed. The <PgDn> and <PgUp> keys can also be used to move vertically one full page at a time, while the <Ctrl+PgDn> and <Ctrl+PgUp> key combinations can be used to move horizontally one full page at a time. Pressing the arrow keys while holding down the <Ctrl> key causes the active cell to be moved to the extremities of the worksheet. For example, <Ctrl+Right> moves the active cell to the IV column, while <Ctrl+Down> moves the active cell to the 16,384th row.

You can move the active cell with a mouse by moving the mouse pointer to the cell you want to activate and clicking the left mouse button. If the cell is not visible, then move the window by clicking on the scroll bar arrowhead that points in the direction you want to move, until the cell you want to activate is visible. To move a page at a time, click in the scroll bar itself, or for larger moves, drag the scroll box in the scroll bar.

When you have finished navigating around the worksheet, press the <Ctrl+Home> keys which will move the active cell to the A1 position. This is known as the 'Home' position. If you press the <Home> key by itself, the active cell is moved to the 1st column of the particular row. Note that there are several areas on your screen; the displayed area within which you can move the active cell is referred to as the working area of the worksheet, while the letters and numbers in the border around the displayed portion of the worksheet form the reference points.

The location of the active cell is constantly monitored by the cell indicator and displayed in the 'status line' which is to be found on the extreme left, below the horizontal 'scroll bar'. If you type text in the active cell, what you type appears in both the 'formula bar', which is to be found below the 'menu bar', and in the cell itself. Typing a formula which is preceded by the equals sign (=) to, say, add the contents of two cells, causes the actual formula to appear in the 'formula bar', while the result of the actual calculation appears in the active cell when the <Enter> key or an arrow key is pressed.

The GOTO Command:
Sometimes it is necessary to move to a specific address in the worksheet which, however, is so far from your present position that using the arrow keys might take far too long to get there. To this end, Works has implemented the **F5** function key as a 'go to' command. For example, to jump to position HZ4000, press the **F5** key, which will cause Works to ask for the address of the cell to which it is to jump. This request appears in a dialogue box.

Now, typing HZ4000 and pressing <Enter>, causes the active cell to jump to that cell address. To specify a cell address, you must always key one or two letters followed by a number. The letters can range from A to IV corresponding to a column, while the numbers can range from 1 to 16,384 corresponding to a row. Specifying a column or row outside this range will cause an error message to be displayed in the dialogue box. To clear the error, press <Enter>, or the <Esc> key; the <Esc> key can also be used to cancel a command and escape from a situation before an error occurs. To return the active cell to the 'Home' (A1) position from wherever it happens to be, press <Ctrl+Home>.

Entering Information

We will now investigate how information can be entered into the worksheet. But first, return to the Home (A1) position by pressing <Ctrl+Home>, then type in the words:

PROJECT ANALYSIS

As you type, the characters appear in both the 'formula bar' and the active cell window.

If you make a mistake, press the <BkSp> key to erase the previous letter or the <Esc> key to start again. When you have finished, press <Enter>. Note that what you have just typed in has been entered in cell A1, even though part of the word ANALYSIS appears to be in cell B1. If you use the right arrow key to move the active cell to B1 you will see that the cell is indeed empty.

Note that the text displayed in the 'formula bar' is prefixed by double quotation marks (") which were added automatically by the program to indicate that the entry is a 'label' and not a number, or a date. Thus, typing a letter at the beginning of an entry into a cell results in a 'label' being formed. If the length of a label is longer than the width of a cell, it will continue into the next cell, to the right of the current active cell, provided that cell is empty, otherwise the displayed label will be truncated.

To edit information already in a cell, move the pointer to the appropriate cell and press the **F2** function key. The cursor keys, the <Home> and <End> keys, as well as the <Ins> and <Del> keys can be used to move the cursor and/or edit the information displayed in the 'formula bar', as required. After such editing of information in the formula bar, you must press the <Enter> key to enter it in the active cell.

Now use the arrow keys to move the active cell to B3 and type

"Jan

Then press the right-arrow key, which will automatically enter the abbreviation 'Jan' into the cell, as a label, and will also move the active cell to position C3. Had we only typed Jan (without the double quotes prefix) on pressing either <Enter> or the right-arrow key, the word 'January' would have appeared automatically in the cell, as a date. In cell C3, type

"Feb

and again press the right-arrow key.

The looks of a worksheet can be enhanced considerably by creating single and double lines, using dashes and equals signs, to separate information in different rows. However, filling active cells with these specific characters, by just typing them repeatedly, causes Works to display an error message and to refuse to accept the entry because they are considered as characters that should precede the entry of a formula.

To fill a block of cells with such characters as dashes, equals signs, or plus signs, you must prefix the characters by double quotes ("). To illustrate this, move the active cell to A4 and type

"==========

(quotes, followed by 10 equals signs - 10 being the default width of a cell). Enter the label into the active cell by pressing <Enter>.

To copy this information to adjacent cells (B4 to C4), mark the range A4 to C4 (from the keyboard use the <Shift+Right>

54

keystroke; with the mouse drag the active cell), then choose the **Edit, Fill Right** command. The equals signs fill the entire marked block of cells, so that a continuous double line appears to stretch from cell A4 through to cell C4.

Finally, type in the label and amounts earned in columns A, B and C of row 5, as shown below.

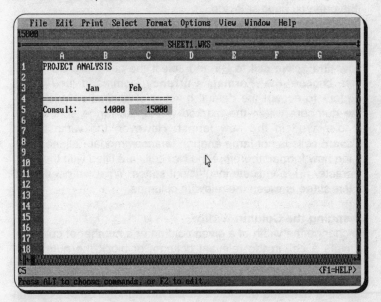

Note how the labels 'Jan' and 'Feb' do not appear above the numbers 14000 and 15000. This is because by default, labels are left justified, while numbers are right justified.

Changing Text Alignment and Fonts:
One way of improving the looks of this worksheet is to also right justify the labels 'Jan' and 'Feb' within their respective cells. To do this, move the active cell to B3 and mark the range B3 to C3 (from the keyboard use the <Shift+→> keystroke; with the mouse drag the active cell), choose the **Format, Style** command, then select the **Right** option listed in the 'Alignment' box of the dialogue box and press <Enter>. The labels should now appear right justified within their cells.

We could further improve the looks of the worksheet by choosing a different font for the heading 'Project Analysis'. To achieve this, move the active cell to A1, choose the **Format, Font** command, then select the Courier, size 7 option, from those listed in the displayed dialogue box, and press <Enter>. Then use the **Format, Style** command, and select the **Italic** option. The heading will now appear in Courier 7, Italic font. Printing or previewing a worksheet can only be done in one font - the one you have selected.

Finally, since the entered numbers in cells B5 to C5 represent money, it would be better if these were displayed with two digits after the decimal point and prefixed with the £ sign. To do this, move the active cell to B5 and select the cell block B5 to C5, then choose the **Format, Currency** command and press <Enter> to accept the default number of decimals, which is 2. The numbers within the marked worksheet range should now be displayed in the new format. However, the width of the relevant cells is not large enough to accommodate all the digits of the new format, therefore the two cells are filled with the hash character (#) to indicate insufficient space. What we need to do at this stage is widen the relevant columns.

Changing the Column Width:
To change the width of a given column or a number of columns, activate a cell in the relevant column, or block the number of required column cells, use the **Format** command and select the **Column Width** option from the pull-down sub-menu. This causes a dialogue box to be displayed with the default column width offered as 10 characters. Typing 12 and pressing <Enter>, changes the width of the relevant columns to 12 characters which allows our numbers to be displayed in their new format. An alternative in this box, new to Version 3.0 of Works is the **Best fit** option, which automatically sets the column width so that the widest column contents are accommodated.

If the currency symbol displays as a '$' don't panic, it just means your version of Works is not set up for the UK. To remedy this, use the **Options, Works Settings** command and select **UK** from the **Country** list box.

Our formatting also produces gaps in the double line below the month headings. To remedy this, use the **F2** function key to enter the 'Edit' mode and add two more equals signs at the end of the A4 entry, then block the cell range A4:C4 and use the

Edit, Fill Right command to correct the entries in cell range B4:C4. Also, change the contents of cell A5 from 'Consult:' to 'Consultancy'.

Saving a Worksheet

At this point, you might like to stop entering information in your worksheet, but would also like to save the work entered so far before leaving the program. You can do this by choosing the **File, Save** command which reveals an appropriate dialogue box. In this box you are offered the default worksheet name SHEET1.WKS as a possible name for saving your work this very first time. Underneath this highlighted field the drive and path are displayed.

You could now type the filename PROJECT1 (which will replace the default name; the extension .WKS is added by Works) and press <Enter>. If you prefer to save your work on a floppy disc in, say, the A: drive, you could include the drive, path and filename (for example, A:\MSWORKS\PROJECT1) which will then become the default until you change it again or start the program afresh. Note that the worksheet name in the title bar changes from SHEET1 to PROJECT1 as soon as you press <Enter> and the file is saved on disc.

```
 File  Edit  Print  Select  Format  Options  View  Window  Help
Consultancy
========================== PROJECT1.WKS ==========================
        A          B          C          D          E          F
 1  PROJECT ANALYSIS
 2
 3                 Jan        Feb
 4  ===============================================
 5  Consultancy £14,000.00 £15,000.00
 6
 7
 8
 9
10
11                                   ▷
12
13
14
15
16
17
18
A5                                                         <F1=HELP>
Press ALT to choose commands; or F2 to edit.
```

57

What you should see displayed on your screen after the above commands have been issued, is shown on the previous page.

At this point you could exit Works and switch off your computer in the knowledge that your work is saved on disc and can be retrieved at any time.

Exiting Works:
To exit Works, use the **File, Exit** command. If you have made any changes to your work since the last time you saved it, an alert box will be displayed on your screen to ask you if you would like to save your work before exiting the program.

Filling in a Worksheet
We will use, as an example on how a spreadsheet can be built up, the few entries on 'Project Analysis' which we used previously. If you haven't saved the PROJECT1 example, don't worry as you could just as easily start afresh.

Retrieving a Worksheet:
If you have saved PROJECT1, then enter the Works program, and choose the **File, Open Existing File** command. Works will display a dialogue box and ask you the name of the file to open with the default file name given as *.*, in the first field of the dialogue box. In the second field, all the appropriate files are displayed. You can select the filename PROJECT1 either by clicking at its name followed by clicking at the **OK** button, or by pressing <Alt+F> to move into the **Files** box, highlight the required file and pressing <Enter>.

Now use the **F2** function key to 'Edit' the existing entries, or simply retype the contents of cells (see the next section for formatting) so that your worksheet looks like the one on the facing page.

Formatting Entries:
Because of the length of some of the labels used and the formatting of the numbers, the default widths of cells in our worksheet were changed from the existing 10 to 12. If you haven't done this already, mark the cell block A1:E1, and choose the **Format, Column Width** command, and type 12 for the new width of the cells, or use the **Best fit** option.

```
 Bld  Ital  Ul    Lft  Ctr  Rt   £  %  ,      Sum    Width    Chart      Prev
=B5+C5+D5
============================= PROJECT2.WKS ================================
         A           B          C          D          E           F
 1  PROJECT ANALYSIS: ADEPT CONSULTANTS LTD
 2
 3                   Jan        Feb        Mar   1st Quart
 4  ======================================================================
 5  Consultancy £14,000.00 £15,000.00 £16,000.00 £45,000.00
 6  ======================================================================
 7  Costs:
 8  Wages         £2,000.00  £3,000.00  £4,000.00
 9  Travel          £400.00    £500.00    £600.00              ▷
10  Rent            £300.00    £300.00    £300.00
11  Heat/Light      £150.00    £200.00    £150.00
12  Phone/Fax       £250.00    £300.00    £350.00
13  Adverts       £1,100.00  £1,200.00  £1,300.00
14                ----------------------------------
15  Total Costs
16                ==================================
17  Profit
```

```
E5                                                               <F1=HELP>
Press ALT to choose commands, or F2 to edit.
```

The information in cell A1

PROJECT ANALYSIS: ADEPT CONSULTANTS LTD

was entered left justified and formatted by choosing the
Forma<u>t</u>, <u>F</u>ont command, and selecting the Courier size 12
options, then choosing the **Forma<u>t</u>, <u>S</u>tyle** command and
selecting the **<u>I</u>talic** option. The labels in the cell block B3-E3
were formatted by choosing the **Forma<u>t</u>, <u>S</u>tyle** command, and
selecting the **<u>R</u>ight** option, so they are displayed right justified.

The numbers within the cell block B5-E17 were formatted by
choosing the **Forma<u>t</u>, <u>C</u>urrency** command, and pressing
<Enter> to accept the default number of decimals.

All the labels appearing in column A (apart from that in cell
A1) were just typed in (left justified), as shown.

Repeated information, like the double line stretching from A4
to E4 was entered by first typing a double quotation mark
followed by 12 equals signs, then marking the block A4-E4, and
choosing the **<u>E</u>dit, Fill <u>R</u>ight** command, which causes the
whole cell block to be filled with the typed character.

Entering Text, Numbers and Formulae:

When text, numbers or formulae are entered into a cell, or reference is made to the contents of a cell by the cell address, or a Works function is entered into a cell, then the content of the message line changes from 'Press ALT to choose commands, or F2 to edit' to 'Press ENTER, or ESC to cancel'. This message can be changed back to the former one by either completing an entry and pressing <Enter> or one of the arrow keys, or by pressing the <Esc> key.

In our example, we can find the 1st quarter total income from consultancy, by activating cell E5 and typing the formula

   =B5+C5+D5

followed by <Enter>. The total first quarter consultancy income is added, using this formula, and the result is placed in cell E5. Note, however, that when cell E5 is activated, the 'formula bar' displays the actual formula used to calculate the contents of the cell.

Complete the insertion into the spreadsheet of the various amounts under 'costs' and then choose the **File, Save As** command to save the resultant worksheet under the filename PROJECT2, before going on any further. Remember that saving your work on disc often enough is a good thing to get used to, as even the shortest power cut can cause the loss of hours of hard work!

Using Functions

In our example, writing a formula that adds the contents of three columns is not too difficult or lengthy a task. But imagine having to add 20 columns the same way! For this reason Works has an in-built summation function (for others see Appendix A) in the form of =SUM( ) which can be used to add any number of columns (or rows).

To illustrate how this function can be used, activate cell E5 and type

   =SUM(

then use the arrow keys to move the highlighted cell to the start of the summation range (B5 in this case), then press colon (:) to anchor the starting point of the range, and use the arrow keys to move the cell pointer to the end of the summation range (in this case D5). What appears against the cell indicator is the entry

SUM(B5:D5

which has to be completed by typing the closing parenthesis (round bracket) and pressing <Enter>.

The Autosum Function:
Another very clever feature new to Works 3.0 is the facility to automatically enter the above =SUM() function into the worksheet. To automatically sum a series of numbers in either a column, or a row, place the active cell where you would normally enter the formula and use the **Edit**, **Autosum** command. Works enters the formula for you; all you have to do is press <Enter> to accept it.

The EDIT, COPY Command:
To copy information into other cells we could repeat the above procedure (in this particular case entering the SUM() function in each cell within the cell range E8 through E13), or we could choose the **Edit, Copy** command, point to the cell block we would like to copy information into and press <Enter>.

To illustrate the copy command, activate cell E5 and choose the **Edit, Copy** command, which causes the information on the message line to change to 'Select new location and press ENTER. Press ESC to cancel'. Move the highlighted cell to E8 and press <Enter>. Then, block the cell range E8:E13 (by either using the <Shift+Down> keystroke or dragging the mouse) and choosing the **Edit, Fill Down** command.

Immediately this command is chosen, its execution causes the actual sums of the 'relative' columns to appear on the target area. Notice that when we activate cell E5, the function target range is B5:D5, while when we activate cell E8 the function target range changes to B8:D8 which indicates that copying formulae with this method causes the 'relative' target range to be copied. Had the 'absolute' target range been copied instead, the result of the various summations would have been wrong.

Now complete the insertion of functions and formulae in the rest of the worksheet, noting that 'Total Cost' is the summation of rows 8 through 13, 'Profit' is the subtraction of 'Total Cost' from 'Consultancy', and that 'Cumulative' in row 19 refers to cumulative profit. Then add another column to your worksheet to calculate (and place in column F) the average monthly values of earnings, costs, and profit, using the =AVG( ) function. The worksheet, up to this point, should look as follows:

```
  File  Edit  Print  Select  Format  Options  View  Window  Help
    Bld  Ital  Ul    Lft  Ctr  Rt    £  %  ,    Sum   Width   Chart      Prev
=AVG(B17:D17)
                            ══ PROJECT2.WKS ══
        A           B           C           D           E           F
  3                    Jan         Feb         Mar    1st Quart    Average
  4
  5 Consultancy  £14,000.00  £15,000.00  £16,000.00  £45,000.00  £15,000.00
  6
  7 Costs:
  8 Wages         £2,000.00   £3,000.00   £4,000.00   £9,000.00   £3,000.00
  9 Travel          £400.00     £500.00     £600.00   £1,500.00     £500.00
 10 Rent            £300.00     £300.00     £300.00     £900.00     £300.00
 11 Heat/Light      £150.00     £200.00     £150.00     £500.00     £166.67
 12 Phone/Fax       £250.00     £300.00     £350.00     £900.00     £300.00
 13 Adverts       £1,100.00   £1,200.00   £1,300.00   £3,600.00   £1,200.00
 14
 15 Total Costs   £4,200.00   £5,500.00   £6,700.00  £16,400.00   £5,466.67
 16
 17 Profit        £9,800.00   £9,500.00   £9,300.00  £28,600.00   £9,533.33
 18
 19 Cumulative    £9,800.00  £19,300.00  £28,600.00                         ▷
───────────────────────────────────────────────────────────────────────────
 F17                                                              <F1=HELP>
 Press ALT to choose commands, or F2 to edit.
```

If you make any mistakes and copy information into cells you did not mean to, then choose the **Edit, Clear** command. To blank the contents within a range of adjacent cells, first mark the cell block, then use the command.

Once you are satisfied that what appears on your screen is the same as what is displayed above, use the **File Save As** command to save your worksheet under the filename PROJECT3, as we shall be using this example in the next chapter.

Quick Key Combinations:
We have already discussed how you can move around a worksheet, edit information in a cell, or mark a range of cells using the pull-down sub-menus.

Another method of achieving these and other operations (some of which will be discussed in the next chapter) is by the use of quick key combinations, which do not require the menu bar to be activated. As you get used to the Works package, you might find it easier to use the quick key combinations which can save you a lot of time.

The following key combinations are for use with the spreadsheet module:

Moving and Selecting

Move right one window	Ctrl+PgDn
Move left one window	Ctrl+PgUp
Move to next named range	Shift+F5
Move to next unlocked cell	Tab
Move to previous unlocked cell	Shift+Tab
Select worksheet row	Ctrl+F8
Select worksheet column	Shift+F8
Select whole worksheet	Ctrl+Shift+F8

Editing

Edit cell in formula bar	F2
Copy contents of cell above	Ctrl+' (apostrophe)
Calculate now	F9
View chart	Shift+F10
View worksheet	F10

Printing a Worksheet

To print a worksheet, make sure that the printer you propose to use was defined when you first installed Works. To check what was installed, choose the **Print, Printer Setup** command. For further details on 'Printer Setup', 'Page Setup', 'Print Preview',

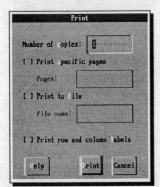

and use of 'Headers and Footers', please refer to the section entitled 'Printing Documents' of Chapter 3. Once a printer has been selected, Works will continue to print to that printer.

To print a worksheet, choose the **Print, Print** command. This causes the dialogue box, shown here, to appear on the screen.

Note that the default settings are 1 copy, all pages, with the printout directed to the printer. You can change any of the options by choosing to print more than one copy, select which pages to print, and direct the output to a file, is so you wish.

Before printing to paper, select the **Print, Preview** command to see how much of your worksheet will fit on your declared size paper, which depends on the chosen font. If the **Preview** option displays only part of your worksheet, and you then direct output to the printer, what does not fit on one page will be printed out on subsequent pages. To fit more of your worksheet on one page, reduce the selected font. Thus, the Preview option allows you to see the layout of the final printed page, which can save a few trees!

Setting a Print Area:

To select a smaller print area than the current worksheet, first block the required area, then choose the **Print, Set Print Area** command. You can now either preview the selected area or print it on paper.

To reset the print area back to the entire worksheet, choose the **Select, All** command, then the **Print, Set Print Area** command once more, before attempting to either preview your worksheet or send the output to the printer.

5. WORKSHEET SKILLS & GRAPHS

We will now use the worksheet saved under PROJECT3 (see end of previous chapter) to show how we can add to it, rearrange information in it and freeze titles in order to make entries easier, before going on to discuss more advanced topics. If you haven't saved PROJECT3 on disc, it will be necessary for you to enter the information into the Works spreadsheet so that you can benefit from what is to be introduced in this chapter. Having done this, do save your work before going on with the suggested alterations. If you have saved PROJECT3, then choose the **File, Open Existing File** command and load the PROJECT3 file. On pressing <Enter>, the worksheet is brought into the computer's memory and displayed on screen.

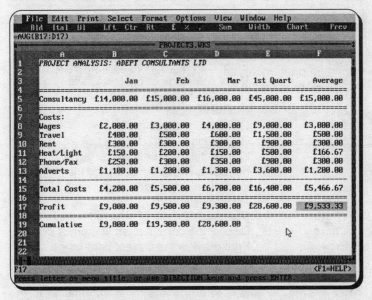

Now use the **Options, Works Settings** command and change the **Lines** option from 25 to 30, which allows five more rows to be displayed on screen. Then, if necessary, use the **Windows, Maximize** command to obtain the display shown above. If you are in Text mode you cannot change the screen display size.

65

The Spreadsheet Toolbar

As with the word processor tool, mouse users of Works 3.0 have an advantage when using the spreadsheet, in that they can make use of the Toolbar. This occupies the second line down of the screen. If you prefer, you can turn it off by activating the **Options**, **Show** command and clicking in the **Show Toolbar** check box. This is a toggle, when the 'X' shows the Toolbar will display, otherwise it will not. The only advantage to be gained by not showing it is you gain one screen line.

To use the Toolbar you simply click the mouse on one of the abbreviated options shown below, and the command selected will be effected on highlighted worksheet cells.

Bld	Ital	Ul		Lft	Ctr	Rt		$	%	,		Sum	Width	Chart	Prev

The meanings of the Toolbar options are as follows:

Option	Result
Bld	Embolden highlighted cell contents
Ital	Make selected cell contents italic
Ul	Underline highlighted cells
Lft	Left align a cell
Ctr	Centre align a cell
Rt	Right align a cell
$	Format selected cells as currency
%	Format selected cells as percent
,	Format selected cells as commas
Sum	Activate Autosum function
Width	Change the width of selected column
Chart	Display the current chart, if there is one
Prev	Print preview the current print range

Controlling Cell Contents

What we will do now is to add some more information to the worksheet with the insertion of another quarter's figures between columns E and F. In fact, we need to insert four columns altogether.

In general, you can insert or delete columns and rows in a worksheet, copy cell contents (including formulae) from one part of the worksheet to another and freeze titles in order to make entries into cells easier.

Inserting Rows & Columns:
To insert columns into a worksheet, point to the column heading where a column is to be inserted and press the left mouse button, which highlights the whole column. Then choose the **Edit, Insert Row/Column** command. Had we highlighted a specific cell, say F1, choosing the **Edit, Insert Row/Column** command would have caused a dialogue box to be displayed, asking you to specify 'row' or 'column' insertion.

Repeat the insertion command three more times so that the column headed 'Average' appears in column J. We could now start entering information into the empty columns, but if we did this first, we would then have to first replicate and then edit appropriately, the formulae used to calculate the various results for the first quarter.

An alternative way is to copy everything from the first quarter to the second and then only edit the actual numeric information within the various columns. We will choose this second method to achieve our goal. First, highlight the cell block B3:E19 and choose the **Edit, Copy** command, then move the active cell to F3 and press <Enter>.

What you will notice immediately is that the cells in row 5, columns F to I, are filled with hashes. The reason for this is that their width is insufficient to hold the numbers that should be displayed in them without truncation. To change the width of the newly inserted columns F to I, use the **Format, Column Width** command, or the Toolbar **Width**, and change the default width of the cells from 10 characters to 12. The width of the highlighted columns are suitably adjusted. Now edit the copied headings 'Jan', 'Feb', 'Mar', and '1st Quart' to 'Apr', 'May', 'Jun', and '2nd Quart'. Save the resultant work under the filename PROJECT4.

Note that by the time the highlighted bar is moved to column J, the 'titles' in column A have scrolled to the left and are outside the viewing area of the screen. This will make editing of numeric information very difficult if we can't see what refers to what. Therefore, before we attempt any further editing, it would be a good idea to use the 'Titles' command ability of Works to freeze the titles in column A and row 1.

Freezing Titles:

To freeze column (or row) headings on a worksheet, move the highlighted bar to the cell below the column (or to the right of the row) you wish to freeze on the screen (in our case B2), and select the **Options, Freeze Titles** command.

On execution, the headings on the said column (and row) are frozen and the highlighted bar cannot be moved into the frozen area. Moving around the worksheet, leaves the headings in such columns (or rows) frozen on the screen. Do this and change the numbers in the worksheet to those below.

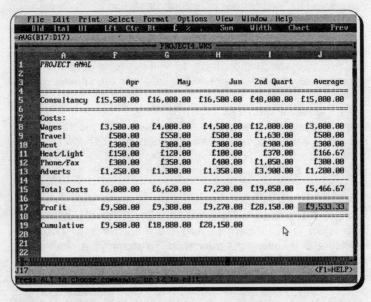

Note: If you examine this worksheet carefully, you will notice that two errors have occurred; one of these has to do with the average calculation in column J, while the other has to do with the accumulated values in the second quarter.

Non-Contiguous Address Range:

The calculations of average values in column J of the above worksheet are wrong because the range values in the formula are still those entered for the first quarter only.

To correct these, highlight cell J5 and press **F2** to edit the formula displayed in the formula bar from AVG(B5:D5) to

AVG(B5:D5,F5:H5)

which on pressing <Enter> changes the value shown in cell J5. Note the way the argument of the function is written when non-contiguous address ranges are involved. Here we have two contiguous address ranges B5:D5 and F5:H5 which we separate with a comma.

Now replicate the formula to the J8:J13 cell range by highlighting cell J5 and choosing the **Edit, Copy** command. Finally, repeat the process for the target cells J15 and J17.

Relative and Absolute Cell Addresses:
Entering a mathematical expression into Works, such as the formula in cell C19 which was

=B19+C17

causes Works to interpret it as 'add the contents of cell one column to the left of the current position, to the contents of cell two rows above the current position'. In this way, when the formula was later replicated into cell address D19, the contents of the cell relative to the left position of D19 (i.e. C19) and the contents of the cell two rows above it (i.e. D17) were used, instead of the original cell addresses entered in C19. This is relative addressing.

To see the effect of relative versus absolute addressing, type in cell E19 the formula

=E5–E15

which will be interpreted as relative addressing. Now, add another row to your worksheet, namely 'Profit/Quart' in row 21, and copy the formula in cell E19 to cell E21, using the **Edit Copy** command. The displayed calculated value in E21 is, of course, wrong (displayed in parentheses) because the cell references in the copied formula are now given as

=E7–E17

as the references were copied relatively.

Now change the formula in E19 by editing it to

=E5-E15

which is interpreted as absolute addressing. Copying this formula into cell E21 calculates the correct result. Highlight cell

E21 and observe the cell references in its formula; they have not changed from those of cell E19.

The $ sign must prefix both the column reference and the row reference. Mixed cell addressing is permitted; as for example when a column address reference is needed to be taken as absolute, while a row address reference is needed to be taken as relative. In such a case, only the column letter is prefixed by the $ sign.

Finally, correct the formulae in cell I19 and I21 in order to obtain the results shown below.

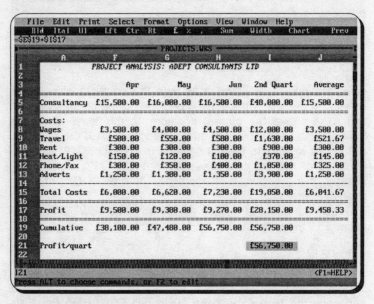

The Edit, Move Command:

To improve the printed output of PROJECT4, we could move the caption to somewhere in the middle of the worksheet. Since the cell whose contents we propose to move is frozen, the move command has to be preceded by additional keystrokes. With the keyboard, first unfreeze the title in column 1 by moving the highlighter to column 2, and choosing the **Options, Unfreeze Titles** command; with the mouse, simply point and click at cell A1 which causes a duplicate of the cell to appear on screen. Now, highlight cell A1 (or its duplicate) and choose the

<u>E</u>dit, <u>M</u>ove command, then highlight cell F1 and press <Enter>. Save the resultant worksheet under the filename PROJECT5.

Multiple Windows

A window can be split into panes which allows the display of different parts of a worksheet as shown below.

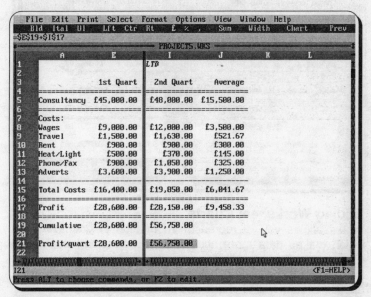

Although this can be done by either using the <u>W</u>indow, Spli<u>t</u> command or by dragging the split bar to the required position, splitting a window vertically, does not allow independent horizontal scrolling. Conversely, splitting a window horizontally, does not allow independent vertical scrolling. Thus, you need to split a window into four panes (the maximum allowable) in order to view greatly separated areas in diagonal panes.

A better method of displaying such areas is with multiple windows. Each window can then be scrolled independently in any direction. As an example of the use of multiple windows, open PROJECT5, save it as PROJECT6 (necessary in order to get an identical copy of the worksheet under a different name), and then open PROJECT5. Now use the <u>W</u>indow, <u>A</u>rrange All command to size the two windows as shown on the next page.

PROJECT5.WKS

	A	E
1		
2		
3		1st Quart
4		============
5	Consultancy	£45,000.00
6		============
7	Costs:	
8	Wages	£9,000.00
9	Travel	£1,500.00
10	Rent	£900.00
11	Heat/Light	£500.00
12	Phone/Fax	£900.00
13	Adverts	£3,600.00
14		============
15	Total Costs	£16,400.00
16		============
17	Profit	£28,600.00
18		============
19	Cumulative	£28,600.00
20		
21	Profit/quart	£28,600.00
22		

PROJECT6.WKS

	A	
1		LTD
2		
3		2nd Quart
4		============
5	Consultancy	£48,000.00
6		============
7	Costs:	
8	Wages	£12,000.00
9	Travel	£1,630.00
10	Rent	£900.00
11	Heat/Light	£370.00
12	Phone/Fax	£1,050.00
13	Adverts	£3,900.00
14		============
15	Total Costs	£19,850.00
16		============
17	Profit	£28,150.00
18		============
19	Cumulative	£56,750.00
20		
21	Profit/quart	£56,750.00
22		

121

<F1=HELP>

Press ALT to choose commands, or F2 to edit.

Adding Worksheet Charts

Works allows you to represent information in graphical form which makes data more accessible to non-expert users who might not be familiar with the spreadsheet format. In any case, the well known saying 'a picture is worth a thousand words', applies equally well to charts and figures.

You can select the charting facility of Works by first selecting a data range to be charted on your worksheet, then choosing the **View, New Chart** command. Works lets you know that you are in 'Charting' mode by displaying the word CHART on the status line. Once this word is displayed, the main menu changes slightly (with the appearance of a **Data** choice in place of **Edit** & **Select**), but most changes are apparent in the sub-menus options. For example, have a look at the options under the **Format** command; they are totally different from those when under the spreadsheet mode. To return to the spreadsheet mode, choose the **View, Spreadsheet** command. The word CHART disappears from the status line and all the main menu choices return to their normal spreadsheet function.

Although Works has only eight two-dimensional chart and graph types, including bar, stacked bar, pie, line and hi-low charts, these can be grouped and overlapped which allows you to add to the list. The eight different main chart-types can be selected from the **Forma_t_** options menu, or from the new Toolbar, after the **_V_iew, _N_ew Chart** command has been selected and the word CHART is displayed in the status line.

To enhance your charts you can add titles, legends, labels, and can select grids, fill types, scaling, fonts, etc. These charts (you can have several per spreadsheet) can be displayed on the screen and can be sent to an appropriate output device, such as a plotter or printer.

The eight main graph-types available are listed below and are normally used to demonstrate the following relationships between data:

Bar   for comparing differences in data - a bar chart displays the values of dependent variables as two-dimensional bars.

Stacked Bar   for comparing cumulative data.

100% Bar   for displaying differences in data as percentages of the total.

Line   for representing data values with points joined by lines and appearing at equal intervals along the x-axis. For such charts, the x-axis could be intervals in time, such as labels representing months.

Stacked Line   for representing the total in each category. A line chart in which the lines are stacked.

Hi-Lo-Close   for showing the extreme high and low values for each point in two or more series of values. This type of graph is useful for showing the high, low, and closing values in trading figures in shares.

Pie   for comparing parts with the whole. This type of graph can display data blocks as slices of a pie. Slices can be shown disconnected or 'exploded' from the rest of the pie.

X/Y   for showing relationships between X and Y. The data points need not appear in equal intervals along the x-axis. Data blocks for such graphs are defined in pairs; each pair consisting of one y-axis block and one x-axis block.

Charts can not be displayed at the same time as the worksheet, but as charts are dynamic, any changes made to the data are automatically reflected on the defined charts.

Preparing for a Bar Chart:

In order to illustrate some of the graphing capabilities of Works, we will now plot the income from consultancies graph of the PROJECT5 file.

First we need to define what we want to chart. However, the specified range of data to be charted must be contiguous for each chart. But in our example, the range of data is split into two areas; Jan-Mar (occupying cell positions B3:D3), and Apr-Jun (occupying cell positions F3:H3), with the corresponding income values in cells B5:D5 and F5:H5. Thus, to create an appropriate contiguous data range, we must first replicate the labels and values of these two range areas in another area of the spreadsheet (say, beginning in cell B23 for the actual month labels and B24 for the values of the corresponding income), as shown below.

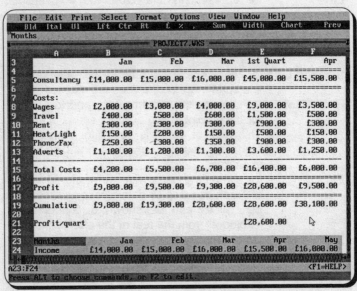

To do this, use the **Edit, Copy** command to copy the labels in the above two cell-ranges into the target area. However, before you replicate the cells containing numeric values, consider what might happen if these cells contained formulae, and you used the **Edit, Copy** command to replicate them. Using this command would cause the relative cell addresses to adjust to the new locations and each formula will then recalculate a new value for each cell which will give wrong results.

The Copy Special Command:
The **Edit, Copy Special** command allows you to copy only cell references without adjusting to the new location. To do this, mark the cell range to be copied (in this case B5:D5) and choose the **Edit, Copy Special** command, then select the **Values only** option from the displayed dialogue box, move the highlighter to cell B24 and press <Enter>. Now repeat the same procedure for the values under Apr-Jun, but copy them into E24 to form a contiguous data range.

Finally, unfreeze the Title protection and add labels for 'Months' and 'Income' in cells A23 and A24, respectively, as shown on the previous page.

The View Command
To obtain a chart of 'Income' versus 'Months', block cell range A23:G24 and choose the **View, New Chart** command. Works clears the screen and draws a bar chart (being the default) of the information contained in the blocked range of cells, as shown on the next page.

When you have finished examining the displayed chart, press <Esc> to display the spreadsheet. Note, however, that the word CHART still appears in the status line. Choosing **View** again, reveals that the chart just displayed on screen appears under the name **1 Chart1** in the **View** sub-menu and is marked with an asterisk to indicate that it is the current chart. To select a different type chart, choose the **Format** command which reveals a sub-menu with all the eight chart types. Note that the **Bar** type has an asterisk against it indicating Chart1's type. You could select another type from the displayed list, but if you do you will lose the Bar chart.

To select another type of chart, but still retain the first chart, activate the **View, New Chart** command, which makes a copy of the current chart as **2 Chart2** and displays it. Press <Esc> to return to the spreadsheet, use the **Format** command and

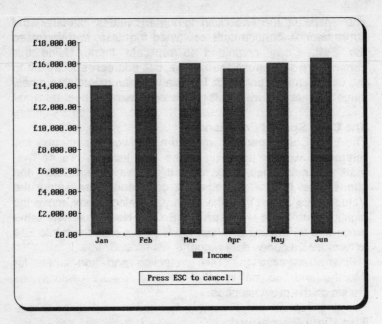

choose the **L**ine option. Now using the **V**iew command and selecting the **2 Chart2** option (which is marked with an asterisk, being the current chart) will draw a line chart on the screen, as shown below.

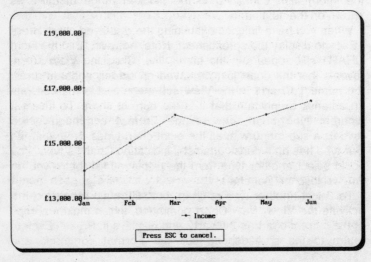

The shape of the line chart was improved by choosing the **Options, Y-Axis** command and typing 13,000 in the **Minimum** box.

There are a lot of other options that you can specify when creating a chart. Some of these are self evident, like titles, legends, data labels, and the inclusion of axis labels and grid lines. These will be discussed only if needed in the examples that follow.

Saving Charts:
Charts are saved with a spreadsheet when you save the spreadsheet on disc. Thus, saving the spreadsheet under the filename PROJECT7, will ensure that your charts are also saved under the same name. Since each chart is linked to the spreadsheet from which it was derived, if information on the spreadsheet changes, the charts associated with it will also change automatically.

Customising a Chart
In order to customise a chart, you need to know how to add titles and axis labels, how to change text fonts, the colour and pattern of the chart, and how to incorporate grid lines.

Drawing a Multiple Bar Chart:
As an exercise, open PROJECT7, if not already in memory, so we can consider a new bar-type chart which deals with the monthly 'Costs' of Adept Consultants. As there are six different non-contiguous sets of costs, you must first copy them (including the cost description labels) using the **Edit, Copy Special** command, into a contiguous range below the 'Income' range (starting, say, at cell A27). Having done this, then copy the 'Months' labels from row 23 to row 26, as shown on the next page, and save the resultant worksheet under the filename PROJECT8.

Now block the cell range A26:G32 and choose the **View, New Chart** command. Immediately this is done, the bar chart of the 6 different monthly costs is drawn automatically for each month in a different colour. The diagram below the worksheet on the next page will appear on your screen, after using the **Print, Format For B&W** command.

Bar   Stk-Bar   100%-Bar   Line   Stk-Line   Hi-Lo   Pie   X-Y   Mixed   Chart   Prev
'Months

	A	B	C	D	E	F
			PROJECT8.WKS			
11	Heat/Light	£150.00	£200.00	£150.00	£500.00	£150.00
12	Phone/Fax	£250.00	£300.00	£350.00	£900.00	£300.00
13	Adverts	£1,100.00	£1,200.00	£1,300.00	£3,600.00	£1,250.00
14						
15	Total Costs	£4,200.00	£5,500.00	£6,700.00	£16,400.00	£6,000.00
16						
17	Profit	£9,800.00	£9,500.00	£9,300.00	£28,600.00	£9,500.00
18						
19	Cumulative	£9,800.00	£19,300.00	£28,600.00	£28,600.00	£38,100.00
20						
21	Profit/quart				£28,600.00	
22						
23	Months	Jan	Feb	Mar	Apr	May
24	Income	£14,000.00	£15,000.00	£16,000.00	£15,500.00	£16,000.00
25	Costs:					
26	Months	Jan	Feb	Mar	Apr	May
27	Wages	£2,000.00	£3,000.00	£4,000.00	£3,500.00	£4,000.00
28	Travel	£400.00	£500.00	£600.00	£500.00	£550.00
29	Rent	£300.00	£300.00	£300.00	£300.00	£300.00
30	Heat/Light	£150.00	£200.00	£150.00	£150.00	£120.00
31	Phone/Fax	£250.00	£300.00	£350.00	£300.00	£350.00
32	Adverts	£1,100.00	£1,200.00	£1,300.00	£1,250.00	£1,300.00

A26:F32   CHART   <F1=HELP>
Press ALT to choose commands, or F2 to edit.

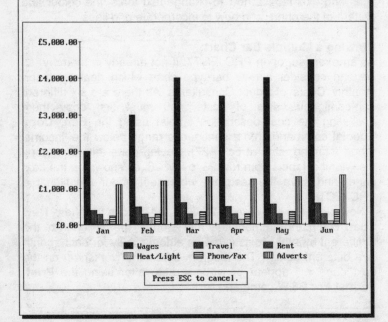

Press ESC to cancel.

78

Chart Titles, Fonts & Sizes:

To add a chart title, choose the **Data Titles** command which causes this dialogue box to be displayed on your screen.

Now type 'ADEPT Consultants' in the **Chart Title** field and 'Monthly Costs' in the **Subtitle** field of the dialogue box and press <Enter>. On choosing the **View** command, both the title and subtitle will appear on screen.

To change the font and size of the newly created title, use the **Format, Title Font** command to display the 'Fonts' and 'Sizes' dialogue box from which you can choose a particular font provided by Works, and change its size by selecting from a list of sizes given in points; a point being 1/72 of an inch.

To change the font of other text and numbers in a chart, choose the **Format, Other Font** command which displays the same dialogue box as the one discussed previously.

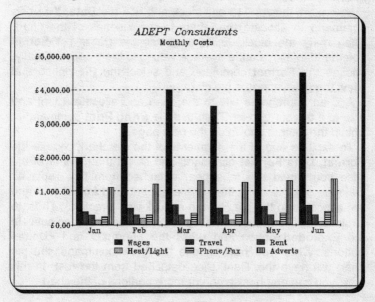

To see the different fonts on screen, choose the **Print**, **Show Printer Fonts** command. Works draws a chart faster when this option is turned off and a chart is displayed using the normal 'screen' font. The fonts and sizes of the text in the chart on the previous page were set as follows:

Chart title: Italic Roman B, size 20
Other text & numbers: Roman B, size 14

Grid lines were added by selecting the **Options**, **Y-Axis** command and activating the **Grid lines** option.

The actual chart shown was printed on paper by using the **Print, Print** command.

Drawing a Pie Chart:
As a second example in chart drawing, use the 'Average' values of the costs from the worksheet of PROJECT8 to plot a pie chart. Again, use the **View, New Chart** command to define a new chart; this could display either the previously defined chart, if cell blocks are still marked in your worksheet, or a 'Series not selected' information box. If a chart is displayed, press <Esc>; if an information box is displayed, press <Enter>. This puts Works in CHART mode.

Now mark the A8:A13 cell block and use the **Data, X-Series** command to allocate the labels to the x-series of the chart. Then mark the block J8:J13 and use the **Data, 1 Y-Series** command to allocate the average values to the y-series. Finally, choose the **Format** command and select the **Pie** option and **View** the newly created pie chart.

Add an appropriate title to the chart and allocate a font and size to it of your choice. Then use the **Print, Print** command to obtain the output shown on the next page.

To explode one of the segments of the pie chart, choose the **Format, Data Format** command and select the number of the slice you would like to appear detached from the displayed dialogue box (slices in this case are numbered from 1 to 6 and are allocated to the pie chart in a clockwise direction). Thus, to explode the 'Rent' slice, select **3** in the **Slices** box, then activate the **Exploded** option and press the <Format> and <Done> buttons. When you now choose the **View** command, the pie chart will have the 'Rent' slice detached from the rest. In this way, you can emphasise one or more portions of the chart.

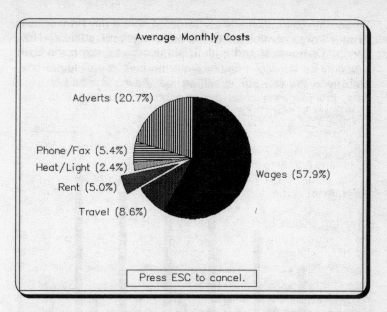

Average Monthly Costs

Adverts (20.7%)

Phone/Fax (5.4%)

Heat/Light (2.4%)

Rent (5.0%)

Travel (8.6%)

Wages (57.9%)

Press ESC to cancel.

To cancel an 'exploded' selection, use the **Format, Data Format** command and press the **Format All** and **Done** buttons. Selecting other slices for exploding, without first cancelling previous selections, adds to the selection.

Mixing Chart Types:
To illustrate a combination of a bar and line chart, we will consider the variable monthly costs of Adept Consultants. This requires us to delete row 29 (the 'Rent' cost, which is fixed) from the worksheet. Just as well, since Works can only deal with a maximum of six categories and we would like to introduce average monthly costs as our sixth category.

Use the **Edit** command to delete the row dealing with 'Rent' from your worksheet; if you are in CHART mode you must select the **View, Spreadsheet** command first. Then, create a new category in the renumbered row 32 to hold the average variable monthly costs.

To create a mixed chart, first enter the CHART mode by using the **View** command and selecting any of the existing charts, then mark the B26:G26 cell block and use the **Data, X-Series** command, then mark the A27:G32 cell block and use the **View, New Chart** command. The chart will look very similar to the

'Costs' bar chart, discussed previously, with a difference; there is no 'Rent' cost, but there is an 'Average/mth' addition. Now use the **Options, Mixed Line & Bar** command, select the **Line L** option for the 6th Y-Series from the revealed dialogue box, and press the **OK** button. When the **View** command is used next, the following chart appears on the screen. Save your worksheet as PROJECT9.

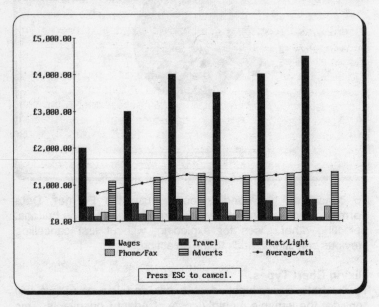

It is possible to display data using two y-axes, by using two different chart types; one type is then displayed on the left y-axis and another type is displayed on the right y-axis. The same thing can also be applied to two sub-groups of the same chart type. To do this, use the **Options, Two Y-Axis** command and specify on the revealed dialogue box which series you want to appear on the left axis and which on the right axis.

6. THE WORKS DATABASE

A Works database is a file which contains related information, such as 'Customer's Names', 'Consultancy Details', 'Invoice No.', etc. A phone book is a simple database, stored on paper. In Works each record is entered as a worksheet row, with the fields of each record occupying corresponding columns.

The next section deals with the basic concepts of using a database, along with the database 'jargon' that is used in this book. If you are not familiar with database terminology then you should read this section first.

A database is a collection of data that exists, and is organised around a specific theme, or requirement. A database is used for storing information, so that it is quickly accessible. In the case of Works, data is stored in **data-files** which are specially structured files that reside on disc like other disc-files. To make accessing the data easier, each row or **record** of data within a database is structured in the same fashion, i.e., each record will have the same number of columns, or **fields**.

We define a database and its various elements as follows:

Database	A collection of data organised for a specific theme
Data-file	Disc-file in which data is stored
Record	A row of information relating to a single entry and comprising one or more fields
Field	A single column of information of the same type, such as people's names
Form	A screen in which one record of data can be entered, displayed, or edited
List	The whole database displayed in a spreadsheet-like format. Multiple records can be entered and edited
Query	A set of instructions to search the database for records with specific properties.

A good example of a database is a telephone directory and, as you will know, to cover the whole country many such paper directories are needed. In the same way, a database can comprise a number of data-files. The following example shows how information is presented in such a telephone directory.

```
Prowse H.B., 91 Cabot Close ........................ Truro 76455
Pruce T.A., 15 Woodburn Road .................. Plymouth 223248
Pryce C.W., 42 North Gate Road .............. St Austell 851662
Pryor A., 38 Western Approach ................. Plymouth 238742
Pryor B.E., 79 Trevithick Road ........................ Truro 74231
Queen S.R., 4 Ruskin Crescent ................. Camborne 712212
Regan R.B., 1 Woodland Avenue ................... Bodmin 78236
```

Information is structured in fields which are identified below, for
a single record, as follows:

Name	Address	Town	Tel No.
Pryor B.E.	79 Trevithick Road	Truro	742310

Creating a Database

A database file, in Works, is created with the **File, Create a
New File** command and then selecting **Database**. This
produces a screen similar to that shown below.

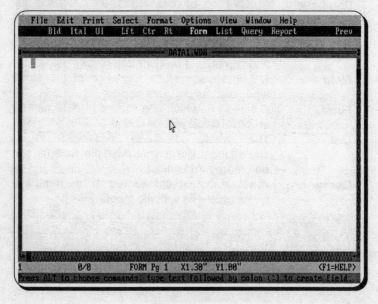

A database file DATA1.WDB is opened as a default. You should not forget to change its name, but without an extension, when you save it. All database files are automatically given the extension .WDB when they are saved.

Database Screens:
As indicated on the status bar this opening screen is a 'Form' window, or view. On it we will build a 'front end' form to enter, and access, our data.

The other way of looking at, and accessing, a Works database is through the 'List' screen, as shown below.

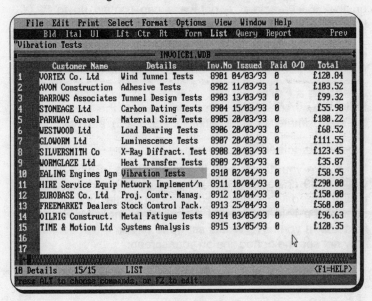

```
   File  Edit  Print  Select  Format  Options  View  Window  Help
        Bld  Ital  Ul    Lft  Ctr  Rt    Form  List  Query  Report          Prev
"Vibration Tests
                            ══════INVOICE1.WDB══════
         Customer Name        Details        Inv.No Issued   Paid O/D    Total
 1   VORTEX Co. Ltd      Wind Tunnel Tests     8901 04/03/93  0          £120.84
 2   AVON Construction   Adhesive Tests        8902 11/03/93  1          £103.52
 3   BARROWS Associates  Tunnel Design Tests   8903 13/03/93  0          £99.32
 4   STONEAGE Ltd        Carbon Dating Tests   8904 15/03/93  0          £55.98
 5   PARKWAY Gravel      Material Size Tests   8905 20/03/93  0          £100.22
 6   WESTWOOD Ltd        Load Bearing Tests    8906 20/03/93  0          £68.52
 7   GLOWORM Ltd         Luminescence Tests    8907 20/03/93  0          £111.55
 8   SILVERSMITH Co      X-Ray Diffract. Test  8908 20/03/93  1          £123.45
 9   WORMGLAZE Ltd       Heat Transfer Tests   8909 29/03/93  0          £35.87
10   EALING Engines Dgn  Vibration Tests       8910 02/04/93  0          £58.95
11   HIRE Service Equip  Network Implement/n   8911 10/04/93  0          £290.00
12   EUROBASE Co. Ltd    Proj. Contr. Manag.   8912 18/04/93  0          £150.00
13   FREEMARKET Dealers  Stock Control Pack.   8913 25/04/93  0          £560.00
14   OILRIG Construct.   Metal Fatigue Tests   8914 03/05/93  0          £96.63
15   TIME & Motion Ltd   Systems Analysis      8915 13/05/93  0          £120.35
16
17
10 Details    15/15      LIST                                         <F1=HELP>
Press ALT to choose commands, or F2 to edit.
```

The above shows the records of a simple database, suitable for keeping track of the invoices issued by a small engineering consulting company. As an example we will go through the stages of setting up this database with the Works package.

As previously mentioned, when a database file is opened, the Form window is shown on the screen. Press **F9**, or Toolbar **List**, or choose **View, List,** to switch to an empty List screen. This gives a spreadsheet type view of the database, with the numbers down the left hand side referring to individual records, and the column headings referring to the database fields. The status line, at the bottom, shows which record the cursor is in, how many records are currently displayed, and how many are in the database.

Use **F9**, or Toolbar **Form**, to change back to the Form window. We will use this window to build a suitable entry form for our database. As it is a multi-page window, the information on the status line is needed to keep track of the current cursor position. The overall maximum form dimensions can be 3 pages long (where each page consists of 5 screen-lengths) by 3 screen-widths wide. A form can contain up to 256 database fields, as well as titles, labels and other text. Each field can hold up to 256 characters. A database can contain up to 32,000 records, which should be enough for most people!

The current cursor position is given on the status line in terms of page numbers, and X and Y co-ordinates in inches, (measured from the top left hand corner of each printed page).

Creating a Form

Move the cursor, either with the mouse, or the arrow keys, to the approximate screen location (X 2.5, Y 2.5), and type

Customer Name:

Make sure you do not omit the colon. Press <Enter>, select a width of 19 characters, and a height of 1 line, in the dialogue box. A dotted line is produced, showing the field location to the right of the field name, and the cursor is moved down to the next line. If you have Works set up to run on a text screen you may not see the dotted line on your screen.

Enter the remaining fields as shown in the table below.

Field Name	Width
Details:	20
Inv.No:	6
Issued:	9
Paid:	4
O/D:	5
Total:	9

You should now have a basic database entry form which looks something like the one shown at the top of the next page.

If you press the **F9** key, or Toolbar **List**, you will see that the List screen now has a row of field titles along the top, above the

```
═══════════════════════════ DATA1.WDB ═══════════════════════════



                                              ↖



     Customer Name: .....................................
     Details: ................................
     Inv.No: ...........
     Issued: ................
     Paid: ........
     O/D: .........
     Total: ................
     ▌
```

```
1        0/0        FORM Pg 1   X2.50"  Y3.67"              <F1=HELP>
Press ALT to choose commands; type text followed by colon (:) to create field
```

darker coloured working area. All of the titles are not, at the moment, visible, as the default column width for a List screen is 10, and some of the fields are longer than this.

These widths can be altered by placing the cursor in the top left cell of the screen, choosing the **Format, Field Width** command, typing **19** in the box and pressing <Enter>. The List screen field widths are in fact independent of those chosen for the Form screen. In our example, we want them to be the same, so alter the other widths as well and then return to the form screen.

Form Editing:

Before entering any records the entry form would benefit from some cosmetic attention. Place the cursor in the cell holding the field title 'Details:' and choose the **Edit, Move Record** command, or **F3** for short. Press the right arrow key six times, and press <Enter>. The field, and its title, have been moved to a new screen location. The top two fields are now lined up on the colon. Move the other fields so that all the colons are in one vertical line.

With the **Edit** sub-menu commands you can move, copy, and delete fields, as well as insert blank lines wherever needed. The

87

editing quick key combinations, given on page 27, and at the end of the chapter, can also be used in the database section.

Place the cursor on the second screen line, at about the position (X 2.9), type the database title

ADEPT CONSULTANTS LTD

and press <Enter>. As there was no colon at the end of the entered text, Works accepts it as a label, not a field. Labels can be placed in any unused space on the form screen. As the title is still highlighted it is a good time to carry out any enhancements. Choose the **Format**, **Style** command, and select **Underline**, from the Style box. Enter the other labels shown in the diagram below.

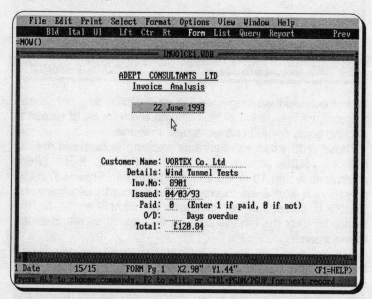

Hiding a Field Name:

The date cell, shown above as 22 June 1993, is not a label. If you look closely you will see the cell has a dotted line below it. It is, in fact, a database field (called Date:), containing a formula to generate the current date, and with its field name switched off.

Place the cursor in the fifth line down, and create a 'Date:' field 17 characters wide. For the moment we will leave this cell

88

empty. To hide it, highlight its field name, and choose the **Format, Show Field Name** command. The field name 'Date:' should now be turned off. If you wanted, you could now place a different label on top of it. This technique is useful if you want to keep actual field names short, but need longer descriptive ones on the front-end form, as with the 'Overdue:' field shown in our previous example.

Entering Data in a Form

We will now enter the first record into the database. Your cursor should be in the date cell. Press <Tab> to move to the 'Customer Name:' field, and type:

Vortex Co. Ltd	press <Tab> and type,
Wind Tunnel Tests	press <Tab> and type,
8901	press <Tab> and type,
4/3/93	press <Tab> and type,
0	press <Tab> twice, and type,
120.84	press <Tab>

Nothing should have been entered in the O/D: field.

The last <Tab> should have completed the entry of record 1, and brought up an empty form for the next record. Press <Ctrl+PgUp>, to move back one record, to the date cell of record 1.

When moving about a form, <Tab> and <Shift+Tab>, move the cursor between fields, whereas <Ctrl+PgUp> and <Ctrl+PgDn>, move between adjacent records.

Using Formulae in a Field:

Database formulae have two main applications; to automatically force the same entry in each similar field of the database, or to calculate the contents of one field based on those of another. Each database field can only contain one formula. Once it is entered in the field of one record, it is automatically entered into all the other records. As in the spreadsheet a formula must always be preceded by an equal sign (=).

In our database example we will enter formulae in two fields, the date formula next, and one that calculates the contents of a field, a little later on. With the cursor in the date cell type

=NOW()

As with the spreadsheet, this formula is shown on the screen, both in the cell and in the formula bar, at the top of the screen. When you press <Enter> a long number should appear in the date cell, but the formula will still be shown in the formula bar. It generates the number of days since the beginning of the century, by using the internal computer clock. Works can use such numbers to carry out mathematical operations using dates.

Formatting Field Cells:
As with a spreadsheet, each field can be given a specific number, or date/time format. A format set in any field of a database record, will force that format for the whole of that database field.

The date number, in our example, can be converted to the current date by changing the format of the cell. With the cell selected, choose the **Format, Time/Date** command, and select **Month,day,year** and **Long** from the dialogue box, to produce the date in the format shown. There are seven different ways to show dates, as well as several 12, and 24 hour time formats. We will leave it to you to explore these other options. If the cell fills with the hash character (#), do not panic, it only means the date is too long for the cell width. Simply alter the cell width with the **Format, Field Size** command. The Total field, on our form, also needs formatting. Select it and choose **Format, Currency,** with 2 decimal places, to show a leading '£' sign.

Locking Fields:
All fields in a Works database are initially locked when first created. These locks, however, only become effective when they are 'activated', with the **Options, Protect Data** command. Not only do these locks prevent the data in a cell from being accidentally altered, but they also cause the <Tab> key to ignore the cell, when you are moving around the form, or entering data.

In our case we need the current date cell to be protected, so we must unlock the other fields, before turning the protection facility on. Select each field in turn, and choose the command combination **Format, Style**, followed by <Alt+k>. At the same time, while in the Style dialogue box, the cell alignments and other styles, could also be changed. When all the fields, except

'Date:', have been unlocked, choose the **Options, Protect Data** command. The date field should now be fully protected. In fact, it is now inaccessible until database protection is toggled off again.

Complete the data entry by typing in the remaining 14 records shown in the screen dump on page 85. When you have saved the database as INVOICE1, a List view should then be the same as that printout.

Sorting a Database:
The records in our database are in the order in which they were entered, with the invoice numbers, in the 'Inv.No:' field, shown in ascending order. However, once records have been entered, you might find it easier to browse through the database if it were sorted in a different way; say, in alphabetical order of 'Customer Name'. This might also make it easier to use the database for other operations, such as a mail merge. Works has an easy to use sort function, which can be accessed from either the Form or List screen.

With the cursor in any location, choose the **Select, Sort Records** command. In the **1st Field** box type the name of the first field to be sorted, in our case **Customer Name**, and select **Ascend** (**Alt+A**). This sorts the field in an ascending order, from A - Z, and from 0 - 9. A descending sort order is the reverse. If you decide to have a secondary sort field (say you want invoices for the same company to appear in ascending order of invoice number), it is a simple matter to define a secondary sort range, before sorting. The three sort ranges available should be enough for most purposes.

Issuing these commands should produce the display shown on the next page.

Now re-sort the database, in ascending order on the 'Inv.No:' field, to return it to the original format.

Date Arithmetic:
There are several date functions which can be used in Works to carry out date calculations. For example, typing the function =DATE(89,4,18) - 18/4/89 backwards - works out the number of days since 31 December 1899. These functions are included to make Works more compatible with Lotus 1-2-3, but Works has an easier, and quicker, way of dealing with date arithmetic.

```
 Bld  Ital  Ul     Lft  Ctr  Rt     Form  List  Query  Report          Prev
"AVON Construction
═══════════════════════════ INVOICE1.WDB ═══════════════════════════
      Customer Name       Details        Inv.No Issued   Paid O/D    Total
 1   AVON Construction  Adhesive Tests      8902 11/03/93  1          £103.52
 2   BARROWS Associates Tunnel Design Tests 8903 13/03/93  0           £99.32
 3   EALING Engines Dgn Vibration Tests     8910 02/04/93  0           £58.95
 4   EUROBASE Co. Ltd   Proj. Contr. Manag. 8912 18/04/93  0          £150.00
 5   FREEMARKET Dealers Stock Control Pack. 8913 25/04/93  0          £560.00
 6   GLOWORM Ltd        Luminescence Tests  8907 20/03/93  0          £111.55
 7   HIRE Service Equip Network Implement/n 8911 10/04/93  0          £290.00
 8   OILRIG Construct.  Metal Fatigue Tests 8914 03/05/93  0           £96.63
 9   PARKWAY Gravel     Material Size Tests 8905 20/03/93  0          £180.22
10   SILVERSMITH Co     X-Ray Diffract. Test 8908 20/03/93 1          £123.45
11   STONEAGE Ltd       Carbon Dating Tests 8904 15/03/93  0           £55.98
12   TIME & Motion Ltd  Systems Analysis    8915 13/05/93  0          £120.35
13   VORTEX Co. Ltd     Wind Tunnel Tests   8901 04/03/93  0          £120.84
14   WESTWOOD Ltd       Load Bearing Tests  8906 20/03/93  0           £68.52
15   WORMGLAZE Ltd      Heat Transfer Tests 8909 29/03/93  0           £35.87
16
17
1 Customer Na 15/15      LIST                            <F1=HELP>
Press ALT to choose commands, or F2 to edit.
```

Just typing a date into a cell, in one of the accepted date formats, allows Works to use the date number in any calculations. When a date is typed in a field, or a spreadsheet cell, what actually shows in that cell depends on the cell format. If '30/10/66', (a date in short date format), is typed into a cell, it will be shown as 30 October 1966 in long date format, or 22219, in any of the number formats.

The function

=NOW()−30/10/66

gives the difference in days (if the appropriate cell is formatted for integer numbers) between now and the mentioned date.

We will use this function to work out the number of overdue days for the unpaid invoices in our example, by typing the following formula into the O/D field cell:

=NOW()−Issued

However, before we proceed, we should take into consideration the fact that, normally, such information would not be necessary if an invoice has already been paid. Therefore, we need to edit the formula to make the result conditional on non-payment of the issued invoice.

The IF Function:

The =IF function allows comparison between two values with the use of special 'logical' operators. The logical operators we can use are listed below.

Logical operators

=	Equal to
<	Less than
>	Greater than
<=	Less than or Equal to
>=	Greater than or Equal to
<>	Not Equal to

The general format of the IF function is as follows:

=IF(Comparison, Outcome-if-true, Outcome-if-false)

which contains three arguments separated by commas. The first argument is the logical comparison, the second is what should happen if the outcome of the logical comparison is 'true', while the third is what should happen if the outcome of the logical comparison is 'false'.

Thus, we can incorporate an =IF function in the formula we entered in the O/D cell, to calculate the days overdue, only if the invoice has not been paid, otherwise '0' should be written into that cell. The test will be on the contents of the corresponding 'Paid' field of a record, and will look for anything else but '0'.

To edit the formula in the O/D cell, highlight the cell and press the Edit key (**F2**). Then press the <Home> cursor key, to place the cursor at the beginning of the existing formula in the formula line at the top of the screen and insert

=IF(Paid=0,

then press the <End> cursor key to move the cursor to the end of the existing entry and add

,0)

The edited formula should now correspond to that shown in the screen printout on the next page.

```
     Bld  Ital  Ul    Lft  Ctr  Rt    Form  List  Query  Report          Prev
=IF(Paid=0,NOW()-Issued,0)
========================= INVOICE3.WDB ===============================
     Customer Name        Details      Inv.No Issued  Paid  O/D   Total
 1  VORTEX Co. Ltd     Wind Tunnel Tests   8901 04/03/93  0   111  £120.84
 2  AVON Construction  Adhesive Tests      8902 11/03/93  1     0  £103.52
 3  BARROWS Associates Tunnel Design Tests 8903 13/03/93  0   102  £99.32
 4  STONEAGE Ltd       Carbon Dating Tests 8904 15/03/93  0   100  £55.98
 5  PARKWAY Gravel     Material Size Tests 8905 20/03/93  0    95  £180.22
 6  WESTWOOD Ltd       Load Bearing Tests  8906 20/03/93  0    95  £68.52
 7  GLOWORM Ltd        Luminescence Tests  8907 20/03/93  0    95  £111.55
 8  SILVERSMITH Co     X-Ray Diffract. Test 8908 20/03/93 1     0  £123.45
 9  WORMGLAZE Ltd      Heat Transfer Tests 8909 29/03/93  0    86  £35.87
10  EALING Engines Dgn Vibration Tests     8910 02/04/93  0    82  £58.95
11  HIRE Service Equip Network Implement/n 8911 10/04/93  0    74  £290.00
12  EUROBASE Co. Ltd   Proj. Contr. Manag. 8912 18/04/93  0    66  £150.00
13  FREEMARKET Dealers Stock Control Pack. 8913 25/04/93  0    59  £560.00
14  OILRIG Construct.  Metal Fatigue Tests 8914 03/05/93  0    51  £96.63
15  TIME & Motion Ltd  Systems Analysis    8915 13/05/93  0    41  £120.35
16
17
3 O/D       15/15      LIST                                    <F1=HELP>
Press letter on menu title, or use DIRECTION keys and press ENTER.
```

Note that once a formula is entered into any one field cell it is automatically copied to all the other cells in that field of the database. Save the file under the name INVOICE3.

Your results will almost certainly differ from those above. The reason for this is, of course, that the NOW() function returns different numerical values when used on different dates. To get the same results as those shown, you could reset your computer clock to that used in our example. This is easily done from within the Works package.

Choose the **File, File Management, Set Date & Time** command, type '23/6/93' and press <Enter>. The <Esc> key will remove the remaining box, but the new date will not be operational, until you leave and re-enter the Works program. Make sure you have saved your work before doing this. When you have finished this section remember to reset the date.

Searching a Database

A database can be searched for specific records, that meet several complex criteria, by the use of the **View, Query** command, or Toolbar **Query**; but for a simple search, on one field only, the **Select, Search** command is both quicker and easier.

We will use the previously saved database INVOICE3 to illustrate both these methods.

Let us assume we needed to find a record, from our database, containing the text 'x-ray'. In the form window, with any record showing, choose **Select, Search,** type **x-ray** in the **Search for** box, and select the option, **All Records**. The record for 'Silversmith Co' is brought to the screen, and the status line indicates that this is the only record that meets the search criterion. To check this press **F9**, to switch to the List screen. Only the one record is shown, and all the others are hidden. The command, **Select, Switch Hidden Records,** will retrieve all the records which did not contain the searched for text. The **Select, Show All Records** command will display the complete database again.

The same search sequence can be carried out in either the Form, or List, windows. In the Form window the whole database is always searched, whereas with List, if a part of the database has been selected, only that part will be searched. Otherwise the whole database is searched, as before.

Database Query:

Sometimes it is necessary to find records in a database that satisfy a variety of conditions. For example, in a warehouse stock database, you may need to find all the items that were purchased between May and July of last year, that were ordered by a specific person, cost between £5.00 and £100.00, and that remained in stock for more than 60 days. In Works this kind of search is called a query.

When a query is carried out in Works, all the records that match the query criteria are displayed. In List view these are all displayed, whereas in Form view you see one matching record at a time. Every time a query is applied the program searches the complete database for matches.

Retrieve the file INVOICE3.DBW, if it is not already loaded, and select the List view. Choosing the **View, Query** command presents a form type screen, with each field left blank. The status line shows us that it is a QUERY view.

Assuming that we would like to search the database for all the details of our customers whose invoices are overdue by 80 or more days, and who owe more than £100, then we would type in the O/D field cell the criterion

>=80

and in the Total field cell the criterion

>100

The screen should now look like that shown below.

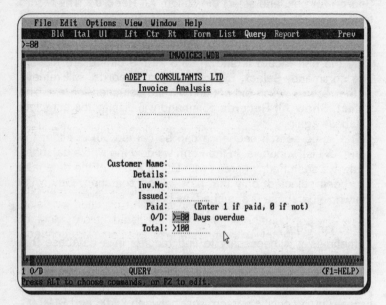

Criteria may be included that refer to one field, or to several fields, of the database (up to 256).

A label, or a value, may be entered exactly as it appears in the database, or the two special characters ? and * can be used, to match any single character of a label, or all characters to the end of the label. Preceding a label with a tilde (~), causes the search of all labels except for that one. Thus, ~Y* searches the database for all records with an entry in that field which does not begin with Y.

To search a database for values, either enter the value as the exact criterion, or use a formula, such as >=80, in which the logical operators (<, <=, >, >=, <>) can be used.

The logical operators AND (&), OR (|) and NOT (~) can be used to link multiple conditions in any query. For example, had we typed the criterion in the O/D cell as >=80&<120 we would retrieve the records that were overdue by between 80 and 120 days.

When all the required criteria have been entered, return to the List view by pressing the **View, List** command. Only the records which meet the search requirements will be listed. In our case this should be three only.

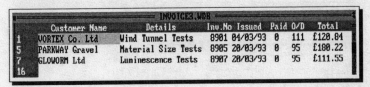

To view all the records again, choose **Select, Show All Records**. The query criteria will remain intact until next edited. Now save this worksheet under the filename INVOICE4.

Quick Key Combinations:
As with the other Works tools several of the editing, selecting and moving menu commands can be short circuited by using quick key combinations. These are all listed below. Most of them are usable only with the database, but some are common to the whole package.

The following key combinations can be used in all the Works tools:

Editing
Move selection   F3
Copy selection   Shift+F3
Repeat search   F7
Repeat copy   Shift+F7
Insert date   Ctrl+; (semi colon)
Insert time   Ctrl+: (colon)

Combinations for use only with the database:

Editing
Edit cell in formula bar   F2
Switch Form/List   F9
View report   Shift+F10
Quit reporting   F10
Apply query   F10

Selecting and Moving - List and Report Views
Select record/row   Ctrl+F8
Select field/column   Shift+F8
Select whole database   Ctrl+Shift+F8
To next unlocked field   Tab
To previous unlocked field   Shift+Tab
Right one window   Ctrl+PgDn
Left one window   Ctrl+PgUp

Moving - Form and Query Views
To next record (Form)   Ctrl+PgDn
To previous record (Form)   Ctrl+PgUp
To next field   Tab
To previous field   Shift+Tab

The Database Toolbar
As with the other tools, mouse users of Works 3.0 have an
advantage when using the database, in that they can make use
of the Toolbar. This occupies the second line down of the
screen. If you prefer, you can turn it off by activating the
Options, **Show** command and clicking in the **Show Toolbar**
check box. This is a toggle, when the 'X' shows the Toolbar will
display, otherwise it will not. To use the Toolbar you simply click
the mouse on one of the abbreviated options shown below, and
the command selected will be effected.

| Bld | Ital | Ul | | Lft | Ctr | Rt | | Form | | List | | Query | | Report | | Prev |

The meanings of the Toolbar options are as follows:

Option	Result
Bld	Embolden highlighted entry
Ital	Make selected entry italic
Ul	Underline highlighted entry
Lft	Left align a field
Ctr	Centre align a field
Rt	Right align a field
Form	Change to form view
Query	Change to query view
Report	Change to report view
Prev	Print preview the current print range.

7. DATABASE APPLICATIONS

Once a database has been created, the data sorted in the required order, and specific records have been searched for, the retrieved data can be browsed on the screen, either one record at a time, or in the list format, one full screen at a time. Some form of hard copy will almost certainly be required at some stage, by printing part, or all, of the database to paper.

Printing from a Database

There are three main ways of printing information from a database. In the 'Form' view, selected records are printed out in the same format as the screen form. Printing from a 'List' view will produce rows and columns just as they appear on the screen; no manipulation of the printed result is possible. To obtain a customised print-out, possibly containing selected fields only, but with report and page titles, totals and sub-totals, a 'Report' must first be defined. Data would then be printed from the Report screen.

From the List window the dialogue box generated by the **Print**, **Print**, or the **Print, Preview**, commands is the same as that described previously in the word processing chapter. This will only produce a usable print-out, if your database has only a few fields per record.

Printing from the Form view could probably be best used with a diary type appointment database, or with a simple database designed to hold, say, personnel lists or parts inventories. Space could be built into each form to hold a photograph on the printed output.

We will leave you to develop these, but to demonstrate the process load the database INVOICE4.WDB, which was created in the last chapter. From the Form view choose **Print**, **Preview** to bring down a dialogue box like that shown on the next page. The command **Print, Print** will also produce this box, but we do not need to print to paper at this stage. We will use the **Preview** feature to see what our print-out would look like.

In the dialogue box, switch off **Page breaks between records**, type '1' as the **Space between records**, and select both **All records** and **All items**. When you press <Enter>, or <Alt+P>, the preview should show three neatly spaced records on the page.

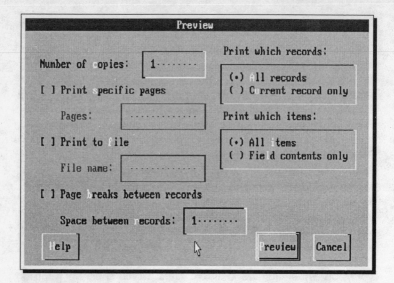

Creating a Report

A report can present records sorted and grouped, with summaries, totals, and with explanatory text. Once a report format has been set up, producing a report is a quick, almost automatic process. The current records 'displayed' in a database are those used to make the body of a report. The initial process is to create a report definition, which indicates what information will be in a report, and where it will be placed. Microsoft have given the Report facility of Works 3.0 a 'semi automatic front end' and the production of simple report formats is now very much easier.

Using the database we built up in the last chapter we will step through the process of setting up a report definition. If necessary, retrieve the file saved as INVOICE4.WDB. This was a database to store details of the invoices sent out by a small company. It would be very useful, for both the accountant and the company management, if a report like that on the next page could be 'instantly' produced, and printed out. This summarises all the unpaid invoices and ranks them in groups depending on the number of months they have been overdue. Once we have defined the format of this report, it will only take a few keystrokes, at any time in the future, to produce a similar but updated report.

```
                    ADEPT CONSULTANTS LTD
                    Invoice Analysis Report

                  Summary of Overdue Invoices

--------------------------------------------------------------
Customer              Invoice       Days          Total
Name                  Number        Overdue        Amount
--------------------------------------------------------------

TIME & Motion Ltd       8915           41         £120.35
OILRIG Construct.       8914           51          £96.63
FREEMARKET Dealers      8913           59         £560.00
--------------------------------------------------------------
1 - 2  Months Overdue     3            51         £776.98
--------------------------------------------------------------
EUROBASE Co. Ltd        8912           66         £150.00
HIRE Service Equip      8911           74         £290.00
EALING Engines Dgn      8910           82          £58.95
WORMGLAZE Ltd           8909           86          £35.87
--------------------------------------------------------------
2 - 3  Months Overdue     4            77         £534.82
--------------------------------------------------------------
PARKWAY Gravel          8905           95         £180.22
WESTWOOD Ltd            8906           95          £68.52
GLOWORM Ltd             8907           95         £111.55
STONEAGE Ltd            8904          100          £55.98
BARROWS Associates      8903          102          £99.32
VORTEX Co. Ltd          8901          111         £120.84
--------------------------------------------------------------
3 - 4  Months Overdue     6           100         £636.43
--------------------------------------------------------------

Overall Totals
and Averages             13            82       £1,948.23
--------------------------------------------------------------
```

Change to the Form screen of INVOICE4.WDB, as we must first add an extra field to the form. This will show the number of months an invoice is overdue. We will need it to provide the basis for sorting the database records, and breaking them up into groups. Open a new field called 'Months:', placed wherever you like on the form, but give it a width of 3.

Highlight the empty cell, type the formula

    =Int(O/D/30)

and press <Enter>. Note that Works places single inverted
commas around the field name O/D, to show it as a label; this is
because it contains the slash character '/'. The formula
produces the integer part of the number of days overdue,
divided by thirty. In other words, the whole number of months
overdue.

We are now ready to create the report definition. Choose the
View, New Report command, or Toolbar **Report**. The New
Report dialogue box is opened as shown below:

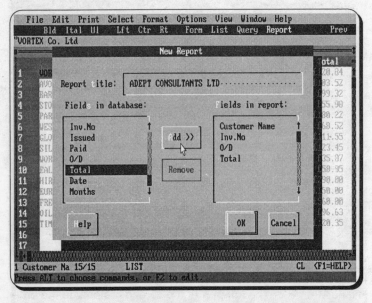

To complete the box as shown, type ADEPT CONSULTANTS
LTD into the **Report title** box. Select the field 'Customer Name'
in the **Fields in database** list box and press **Add**, or <Alt+A>,
to add the field to the **Fields in report** list. In the same way add
the fields 'Inv.No', 'O/D' and 'Total' and then choose **OK** to
select the dialogue box options.

The Report Statistics box is then shown. This provides a
quick way of entering formulae into the report, to carry out
calculations and produce totals or averages for example. In the

future you should find this an easy way to generate rapid reports, but at this stage we will not use this method, so press **OK** to move to the next screen, which gives a rough indication of what your report will look like.

The message line at the bottom of the screen tells you to "Press ENTER to continue, ESC to cancel". At the moment these are the only two keys that will operate. Press <Enter> several times to page through the 'report', until the report definition screen below is obtained.

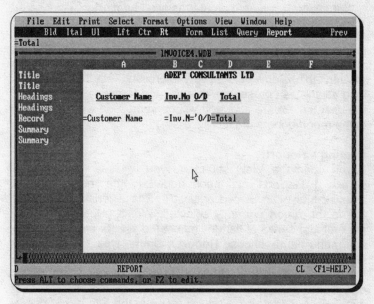

The working area of the screen, contains columns and rows which intersect, as in a spreadsheet, to form cells. The row types, shown on the left part of the screen, determine the order the rows will be printed in the report, and what action will be taken in that row, as shown below:

Row type	Prints
Title	At the beginning of a report
Headings	At the top of each page
Intr *1st breakfield*	At the beginning of each group created by the 1st breakfield
Intr *2nd breakfield*	At the beginning of each group created by the 2nd breakfield

Intr *3rd breakfield*	At the beginning of each group created by the 3rd breakfield
Record	Each displayed database record
Summ *3rd breakfield*	At the end of each group created by the 3rd breakfield
Summ *2nd breakfield*	At the end of each group created by the 2nd breakfield
Summ *1st breakfield*	At the end of each group created by the 1st breakfield
Summary	At the end of a report

At this stage the 'Intr' and 'Summ' line types do not appear on our screen, as there are no breakpoints defined for the report.

If you printed the report generated from this initial procedure we don't think you would be very impressed with the results. As long as you can persevere, though, and follow us to the end of the chapter, we are sure you will be impressed with the power of the report generating facility.

Naming a Report:
If you open the **View** sub-menu you will see that a report named **1 Report1** has been added to the menu, and an asterisk has been placed against it. The asterisk means that this is the report currently selected. Works gives any reports generated a series of names, numbered 1, 2, 3, etc. To change this menu name, choose **Reports, Name**, type 'Overdue' and select **Rename, Done**. The **View** sub-menu should now contain the option ***1 Overdue**. When a database is saved, any report definitions generated are saved with it, including sorting instructions. Obtaining a similar report in the future is simply a matter of selecting it from the **View** sub-menu.

Defining a Report:
The definition to automatically produce the report on page 101 is shown in the next screen dump example. This was designed to print on an A4 sheet of paper, with 1" margins.

As an example we will go through the procedure of producing this report. Most of the reporting features should become apparent during the operation. You may also find it useful to spend a few minutes with the relevant section of the Works tutorial.

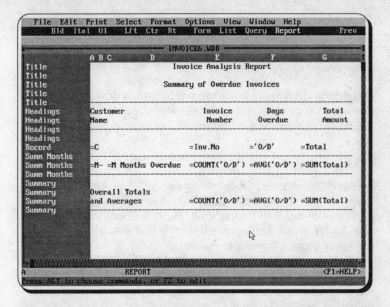

The report definition will be easier to prepare from an empty work area, so choose **S̲elect, A̲ll** and then **E̲dit, Cle̲ar** to clear the working area cells.

The first operation is to reset the column widths. Set columns A, B and C to a width of 2, by selecting these columns, choosing **Forma̲t, Column W̲idth** and typing 2, followed by <Enter>. In the same way, alter the other columns as follows: D to 17, E to 14, F and G to 12.

Adding a Report Title:

The 'Title' rows hold any text that is to appear at the top of the first printed page of the report. In our example we will need six rows of this type, so we must insert four more. Press <Ctrl+Home> to move the cursor to the Home cell, highlight the top two cells of row A by pressing, **F8** followed by the down arrow, choose **E̲dit, I̲nsert Row/Column** and select **R̲ow** in the dialogue box. The next box asks what type of rows are to be inserted; we want 'Title', which is highlighted, so press <Enter> to complete the operation. As we highlighted two rows initially, two new ones should have been inserted. Repeat the operation to insert a further two rows, making six in all.

To position the main report title in the centre of the printed page, move the cursor to column D of the top row, press the space bar 14 times, type

ADEPT CONSULTANTS LTD

and press <Enter>. We will leave it to you to add the other two title lines on rows 2 and 4. To place the horizontal line across the page, position the cursor in A6 (column A and row 6) and type

"--------------------

followed by <Enter>. Copy this to every cell of that row across the screen, with the **Edit, Copy** command. Note that the line in each cell is actually longer than the actual cell widths. In this way if you widen any of the columns in the future you should not get any gaps forming in the line.

Adding Page Titles:
Page titles are placed in 'Headings' type rows, and appear below the report title on the first page of a report, and at the top of all subsequent pages. We will need four of these type of rows, so insert two more, as described earlier. The top two of these rows will hold the four report column titles, as shown on page 101. To enter these, place:

Customer and Name	- left aligned	-	in column A
Invoice and Number	- centre aligned	-	in column E
Days and Overdue	- centre aligned	-	in column F
Total and Amount	- right aligned	-	in column G.

The easy way to select the above alignments is by clicking the relevant options on the Toolbar. In fact, the Toolbar is the only way of checking the actual alignment of a cell's contents. The alignment type of a selected cell will show in white on the Toolbar.

To copy the line from row 6 to row 9, place the cursor at A6, press **F8** to start selecting, press <End> to highlight the line, choose the **Edit, Copy** command (**Shift+F3**), move the cursor to A9 and press <Enter>.

Using Formulae in a Cell:

The body of the report will be produced by the contents of the 'Record' row. If we type a fieldname, preceded by an equals sign, in a 'Record' cell, Works places the contents of that field for each record into the report.

There are also a series of statistical operators that can be included in cell formulae. These are mainly used in 'Summ' type rows, to produce totals, averages, etc. When placed in a 'Summ fieldname' row they give field statistics for the previous group printed. In a 'Summary' row the statistics refer to that field for the whole report.

Statistic	Calculates
SUM	Total of the group
AVG	Average of the group
COUNT	Number of items in the group
MAX	Largest number in the group
MIN	Smallest number in the group
STD	Standard deviation of the group
VAR	Variance of the group

There are several ways to enter formulae in a cell. If you can remember all your database fields, the easiest is probably to simply type the formula in.

The **Edit, Insert Field Name** and **Edit, Insert Field Contents** dialogue boxes list all the fields of the database.

The **Edit, Insert Field Summary** box lists not only the database fields, but all the above statistical functions, which you can select to place in a 'Summ' type row.

In our example, to complete the 'Record' row, simply type the following formulae into the cells shown below and format the cells as follows:

Cell	Contents	Style	Format
A	=Customer Name	Left justified	
E	=Inv.No.	Centre justified	Fixed (0)
F	=O/D	Centre justified	Fixed (0)
G	=Total	Right justified	Currency (2)

Sorting a Report:

A report is sorted to arrange the database entries in a certain order, such as alphabetically or by date. A sort order specified in a report stays with that report, until it is physically changed.

The main sort field, in our case, is on the Months field. We must specify the sort parameters now, as 'Summ' type rows cannot be used without a breakpoint having being entered.

The **Select, Sort Records** command will produce a dialogue box similar to that below. The selections shown are those required for our example. To obtain them, type Months in the **1st Field**, select an **Ascending** search and force a break, <Alt+G>, on this field.

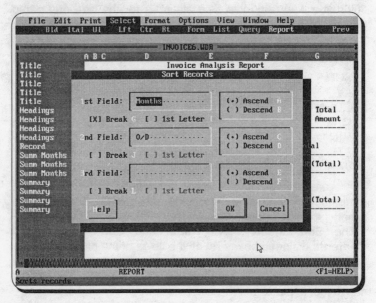

This will cause the report to split its output every time the value of the field 'Months' changes. In our case, for neatness, we have also specified a **2nd Field** ascending sort on the O/D field. If our database contained many hundreds of records, with several for each customer, we could also sort, and break, on the Customer Name field. A summary for each customer would then be produced.

When the sort dialogue box is accepted, an extra row, 'Summ Months', is placed in the report definition. Note that a series of simple formulae is also inserted in this new line. In our case, most of these are not a lot of use, as can be demonstrated by looking at the report so far produced.

From the definition screen this can be done with the key combination <Shift+F10>, while pressing <Esc> will return you to the previous screen. Clear the formulae in columns A to F, with the **Edit, Clear** command, but leave that in G which we will use below.

Completing the Report Definition:
Insert two more 'Summ Months' rows, and enter the following formulae in the middle row cells, with the formats and styles shown.

Cell	Contents	Style	Format
A	=Months	General	Fixed (0)
B	"–	General	
C	+Months+1	Right justified	Fixed (0)
D	" Months Overdue	General	
E	=COUNT('O/D')	Centre justified	Fixed (0)
F	=AVG('O/D')	Centre justified	Fixed (0)
G	=SUM(Total)	General	Currency (2)

When you have completed this row copy horizontal lines, as described previously, and place them both above and below it.

Our report definition is almost complete now, only the 'Summary' rows remain to be done. If you have worked your way to this stage, entering these rows on your own should present no problems.

Insert two more 'Summary' type rows. Leave the top one blank, place a line in the bottom one, and type the following in the remaining two rows:

Cell	Contents	Style	Format
Row 16			
A	Overall Totals	Left justified	
Row 17			
E	=COUNT(O/D)	Centre justified	Fixed (0)
F	=AVG(O/D)	Centre justified	Fixed (0)
G	=SUM(Total)	Right justified	Currency (2)

Applying a Query:
For a report to show the correct records, the database must first be searched using the required retrieval criteria, as was described in the previous chapter.

In our case the report should include all the invoices which have not been settled. Choose the **View, Query** command, type a zero in the Paid field, and press <Enter>. The correct records should now be active. Use the Toolbar **List** option to jump to the List view and check that the Query has worked.

Printing a Report:
To look at the report on the screen press <Shift+**F10**>, or Toolbar **Report**. If you were not satisfied with something, you could press <Esc> to return to the definition screen to carry out any fine tuning required. Printing a report is the same as printing a word processor document, except that the facility to force column page breaks is included, as is the case with spreadsheets. Choose **Print**, make sure your page is set up with 1" margins, and select **Preview** to see what your report will look like on paper. It should be similar to the screen dump shown below. Press **P** to start printing, or <Esc> to cancel the operation.

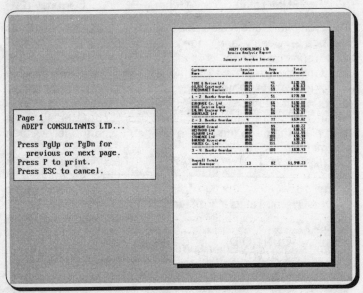

Form Letters

We are now in a position to use the mail merge capability of Works to create customised 'form letters', which make use of information stored in a database. As an example of this, we could create the following simple database which contains the personal details of our potential customers. Save it as ADDRESS.WDB.

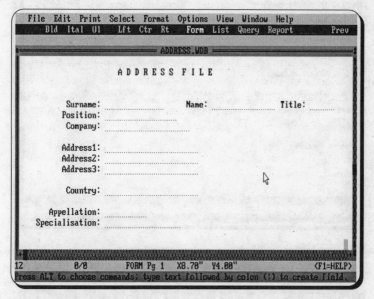

Now type the letter shown on the next page, using the word processor. Note the way the various field names are enclosed by angled brackets. These 'field name markers' cannot be just typed in place. Move the cursor to where you want a field name marker and choose the **Edit, Insert Field** command. In the Database box select the file name of the database to use, in our case ADDRESS.WDB. In the fields box select the field name you want and press <Enter>. Works will place the field name in the document. When the letter is completed save the document as LETTER.WPS.

Note the field 'Appellation' which could be 'Sir', if you didn't know the name of the recipient, 'Mr Brown', if you did or 'John', if he was a friend of yours.

The field 'Specialisation' is included so that your form letters are only sent to relevant people. You would use information in this field in a Query to select records.

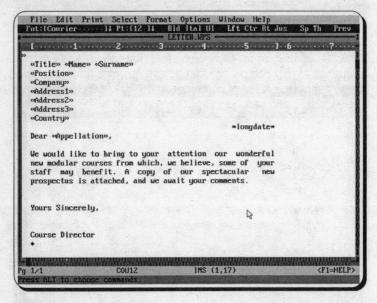

Printing Form Letters:
Works will print one copy of the letter for each record displayed in the database. Before continuing make sure the database has been searched and sorted to display the records you need.

Open both the database file and the file holding the form letter. In our case ADDRESS.WDB and LETTER.WPS. From the word processor file, make sure your printer is set up correctly, choose **Print, Print Form Letters**, select the database to use in the database box, press <Enter> and finally complete the usual Print dialogue box for **Number of copies**, etc. You could of course use the **Print, Preview** command first to check the paper set-up.

That is all there is to it. As long as you do not run out of paper, Works will print as many letters as there are records selected. To stop the operation press <Esc>.

This procedure is not, of course, restricted to producing letters. It can be used for any word processed document which extracts information from a database.

8. USING MACROS

A macro is a set of instructions made up of a series of keystrokes and commands that you would normally type from the keyboard, but which you type instead into a macro generator, which stores the keystrokes in a special file. After entering a macro in this way, and allocating a keystroke sequence to it, it can be invoked by simply pressing those keys. Thus, a macro is a list of commands which is used to perform a specific task, and can be used whenever you wish to save time in performing repetitive commands. Macros can be used in any of the Works tools.

Creating a Macro

We will now use the spreadsheet saved as PROJECT3 (see the beginning of the 'Worksheet Skills & Graphs' chapter) to show how we can add macros to it. Our macro will perform a simple 'what-if' type projection, by increasing the 'Wages' bill by 15%.

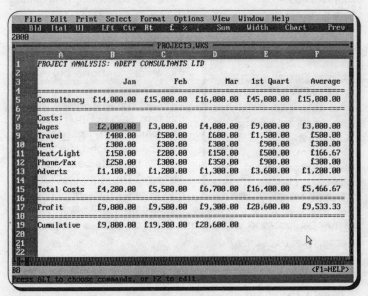

If you haven't saved PROJECT3 on disc, it will be necessary for you to enter the information shown above so that you can benefit from what is to be introduced. Having done this, save it under PROJECT3 before going on.

If you have saved PROJECT3, then enter Works and use the **File, Open Existing File** command to load the file. What should appear on screen is shown on the previous page.

What we would like to do now is to 'Edit' the entries under 'Wages' so that this part of the costs can be increased by 15%. We can then see what overall effect this has on the company figures. One way of doing this would be to multiply the contents of each cell containing the 'wages' value by 1.15. To do this, we would start by 'editing' the contents of cell B8 by pressing **F2** to 'Edit' the value in it, placing an equals sign at the beginning, and adding '*1.15' to the end. This has the effect of multiplying the contents of the cell by 1.15 which would increase its contents by 15%. We would then press 'Enter', press the Right arrow key to move to C8 and repeat the whole procedure.

To carry out a repetitive procedure like this on a series of cells would be very boring, but would be an ideal application for a simple keystroke macro. The exact steps, after highlighting cell B8, could easily be recorded as a macro, which could then be used to change the contents of other cells.

To get into Works macro mode press <Alt+/> which brings up the **Macro options** box shown alongside.

Select **Record Macro** from this box, press <Ctrl+P> as the **Playback key** (P for percent), give the macro the title 'Times 15%' in the **Title** box and press <Enter>. The word RECORD now shows on the right of the message line. All key strokes will now be recorded until either <Alt+/> or <Alt+–> are pressed.

Press **F2** to 'Edit' cell
Press **<Home>** and type =
Press **<End>**
Type ***1.15**
Press **<Enter>**
Press **Right arrow**
Press **<Alt+/>**

Pressing the final <Alt+/> brings up the **Macro options** box again, but this time with a different set of options, as shown here.

Note that the message RECORD still shows on the screen until you select **End Recording** from the box. Our simple macro is now saved.

Before executing any macro, save your worksheet, in this case under the filename MACRO1. This is a simple precaution, if things go wrong your macro could damage your worksheet, and it is usually easier to reload the worksheet and edit the incorrect macro than to have to correct the worksheet!

To use the macro, highlight the next cell to be updated (in this case C8) and press <Ctrl+P>. Watch the changes that take place in the adjacent cells. The highlight should be moved to cell D8; run the macro again to complete the changes to this row.

Works stores macros in the file MACROS.INI which must be in the same directory as the program files. To look at how the macro is stored use the **File, Open Existing File** command to retrieve the MACROS.INI file into the word processor. The contents of the file should look like the following:

```
                                              MACROS.INI
L · · · · · · · · · 1 · · · · · · · · · 2 · · · · · · · · · 3 · · · · · · · · · 4 · · · · · ·
» *Times 15%
  <begdef><ctrlp>
  <f2><xhome>=<xend><k*>1.15<enter>
  <xright>
  <enddef>

  ◆
```

When you become proficient with the use of macros it is possible to write them straight into this file. Every macro must have an * on the title line, must start with <begdef> and must end with <enddef>. While the MACROS.INI file is open the use of actual macros is suspended, so close the file and return to the spreadsheet.

We could use the same macro to increase the other costs by a different percentage, by editing it, but this would be rather inefficient. A better method would be to allocate a cell for the % increase, say cell H8, and re-enter the macro so that reference to that cell is made in absolute terms. For example, in cell H7, type

Increment

and in cell H8 type the actual % increase (in the previous case this would have been 0.15). Now format cell H8 with the **Format, Percent** command, or use Toolbar **%**, accepting the default 2 decimal places. Finally highlight the cell B8, replace its contents with 2000, C8 with 3000 and D8 with 4000. The sheet should now have its original figures. Re-enter the macro, again as <Ctrl+P>, as follows:

Press **F2** to 'Edit' the cell
Press **<Home>** and type =
Press **<End>**
Type *(1+h8)
Press **<Enter>**
Press **Right arrow**
Press <Alt+/>

The highlight bar should be on cell C8, press <Ctrl+P> twice to test the macro. The 'Wages' row should now have been increased by 15%.

Now change the value in cell H8 to 0.20, to attempt to increase the next row by an additional 20%. You will notice in fact, that as soon as you change the contents of H8, the actual values in cells B8..D8 also change to reflect this new change. This is because we have left these cells with formulae in them, which change the cell contents whenever cell H8 is changed.

This, of course, will inevitably lead to errors, unless we incorporate the **Edit, Copy Special** command within the macro. This command copies the contents of cells from one range to another and converts formulae to generated values. In our case we will copy the range to itself, thus 'fixing' the numerical values.

Place the following additional keystrokes into the above macro before the 'Press **right arrow**' line:

> Choose the **Edit, Copy Special** command
> Press **<Enter>**
> Select **<Alt+V>**, and press **<Enter>** again

You should now have a macro that will easily increment any worksheet cell by the amount previously entered in the increment cell (H8).

Range Names
It is a very good idea to give range names to appropriate cells in a spreadsheet, so that reference to such cells can be made by range name rather than discrete cell addressing.

The above macro would only be usable on another spreadsheet if that sheet had 'increment' values also entered in cell H8. If the increment cell had been named, and the macro set to reference the name, not the actual cell, the macro would be much more flexible.

To name a cell, or a block of cells, first select the range to be named, cell H8 in the above case, and then use the **Edit, Range Name** command, if necessary, type the name, in our case 'increment' is already suggested by the program, and select **Create**.

Another use of range names is that you can 'jump' to them from anywhere in the worksheet by using the **F5** (Goto) command. To add this facility to the above <Ctrl+P> macro we will recall and edit the macro storage file MACROS.INI. When opened in the word processor this file should contain the following:

```
                              MACROS.INI
 L. . . . . . . .1. . . . . . . .2. . . . . . . .3. . . . . . . .4. . . . . . . .5
» *Times 15%
   <begdef><ctrlp>
   <f2><xhome>=<xend><k*>(1+$h$8)<enter>
   <mcnu>cs<cntcr>
   <altv><cntcr>
   <xright>
   <enddef>

   ♦
```

Note that Works saves each menu command sequence on a separate line, to make it a little easier to understand what the macro is meant to do. On the second line of the macro text, place the cursor on the 'h' between the two '$' signs, delete 'h$8', and type in its place the range name 'increment'.

Once you can work out how the program stores its macros, it is far easier to modify them by editing the code, than it is by re-recording the macros. Save the modified document with the **File, Save** command and clear MACROS.INI from the screen with the **File, Close** command.

Macro Interaction

A final addition to the above macro could be made to allow for user entry of the 'increment' value from the keyboard, rather than having to edit cell H8.

Fixed Input Pauses:

This can be achieved by selecting **Fixed Input** from the **Macro options** dialogue box, which allows the user to enter a prescribed number of keystrokes whenever it is encountered in a macro.

To use this, instead of typing '$increment' on the formula line when recording the macro, type '.', press <Alt+/> to bring up the **Macro options** menu, select **Fixed Input** and type a sample of the required input. In the above case this would be '15' - for 15%. To end the fixed input type <Alt+/> again, choose **OK**, and complete the macro entry as before.

In fixed input, Works keeps track of the number of keystrokes, and when the macro is played it pauses until that number of keys are pressed, and then continues.

When generating macros two other types of pauses can be used, timed and variable-input pauses. Like the fixed input pause these are both placed into a macro from the **Macro options** menu.

Timed Pauses:

These cause the macro to pause for a certain time, before continuing with its operation. From the **Macro options** box select **Pause** and type the required pause time in the format: - HH:MM:SS.T. Thus 1 hour 15 minutes 25.6 seconds would be entered as: - '1:15:25.6' (without the apostrophes).

When a macro is run, it will stop operation, when it reaches the pause, for the specified time. Pressing any key during the pause period will cancel the remainder of the pause and restart the macro. A pause could thus be built into a macro doing a repetitive operation to give you a chance to stop it, if necessary.

Variable Input Pauses:
When a variable input pause is placed in a macro, by selecting **Variable Input** from the menu box, the macro is paused to accept interactive keystrokes from the operator. It restarts whenever <Enter> is pressed. This would be used to input spreadsheet, or database cell contents, or enter text into a word processor macro.

Nested Input Macros:
A nested input macro allows you to pause a macro and type variable input (as described above). This input however, is given a macro name of its own, and becomes a separate macro which can be repeated, any number of times, from within the main macro.

Some Word Processing Macros:
We have been impressed with the Works package since Version 2.0 was released and Version 3.0 is even better. However, when moving from another package there are always certain features which you look for. In our case the Works word processing delete options seemed a little sparse. This does not matter, however, if a package has a macro generating facility. It is just a matter of assigning the missing editing options to suitable key combinations.

The following are the keystrokes of several small, but useful, macros that we use regularly:

To delete the word at the cursor

    <Ctrl+BkSp>   Press **F8** twice to select the word
                              Press **<Del>** to delete it

To delete from cursor to end of line

    <Alt+End>   Press **F8**, **<End>**, **<Del>**

To delete a whole line

<Ctrl+Y>   Press **F8, F8, F8, <Del>**

If after you have recorded several macros you forget the key combinations, or you decide that you want to change them, simply call up the **Macro options** menu and work your way through the other choices on it.

Skipping a Macro:
This option is the only one on the menu that is not self explanatory. With Works you can assign most keys to macros, but Works itself uses many such combinations for menu short cuts, editing commands etc. If a macro has been assigned such a Works' key combination, you can press **Skip Macro**, (or ` , the accent grave key for short) and use the playback key for its original Works function.

9. OTHER WORKS FEATURES

The Calendar
New to version 3.0, the Calendar is a useful tool that can help you keep track of all your appointments, birthdays and anniversaries. In short, it can help you organise both your personal and your working life. Being part of an integrated package, like Works, you can keep your calendar file open all day, so it will always be there to use.

To access the function press the **Open the Calendar** button in the opening screen dialogue box, or, from within Works, use the **Options**, **Calendar** command. Both methods will initially open the following blank screen.

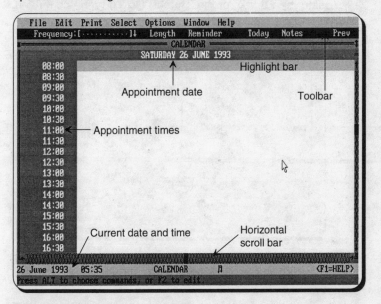

Moving Around the Calendar:
The first time you open the Calendar the current system date is shown at the top immediately below the title bar. This is the 'Appointment' date and a screen of times and places to enter appointments goes with it. There are several ways to change this date, or as it were, to page through the diary.

121

From the keyboard

Press <Ctrl+→> or <Ctrl+←> to move forward, or backward, one day at a time.
Press <Ctrl+PgDn> or <Ctrl+PgUp> to move forward, or backward, one week at a time.

With the mouse

Click the right and left arrows at the end of the horizontal scroll bar, to move forward and backward one day, or
Click the scroll bar itself, to move one week at a time. Click to the left of the centre box to move back one week, and to the right to move forward.

Using Go To

Pressing the **F5** key, or the **Select**, **Go To** menu command, will open the following box.

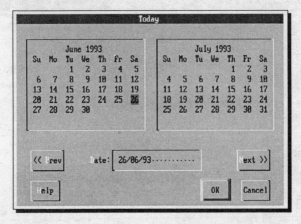

This shows a two month calendar display with the current date highlighted and placed in the **Date** box. You can move rapidly to another date by clicking it with your mouse and pressing <Enter>. Select << **Prev** to show one month earlier, or >> **Next** to show one month later. Alternatively, you could type any date (in the format shown above) into the **Date** box and press <Enter> to jump to that date.

Notice that the appointment date changes but the current date, shown above and to the left of the status line, obviously remains the same. To use your Calendar effectively you should make sure your system date is set correctly (See page 94).

To return the calendar page to the current date either press <Ctrl+T>, or use Toolbar **Today**.

Changing Appointment Times:

By default these are shown at half hourly intervals down the left side of the screen. You may prefer to reset the interval to one hour. If this is so, use the **Options**, **Appointment Times** command from the menu bar, select **1 hour**, as shown here, and press <Enter>, or select **OK**.

Entering Appointments:

To enter an appointment move the highlight bar to the correct time, either with the mouse, or by pressing direction keys.

With the mouse, click the start time required for the appointment. If it is not visible on the screen, use the vertical scroll bar to move up and down through the day's schedule.

With the keyboard use the ↑ and ↓ arrow keys to move one appointment at a time, the <PgUp> and <PgDn> keys, to move one screen at a time, or the <Home> and <End> keys to move to the start, or end, of the days calendar.

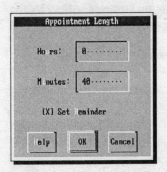

Then simply type in the details of the appointment, as you would write them in your planner, or your diary. When you press <Enter>, to fix the text, the box shown opens so that you can fix the length of the appointment. You can enter either **Hours**, **Minutes** or a combination of both. If you select **Set Reminder**, as shown, Works will remind you of your appointment 5 minutes before its start. For this to work you must, of course, have the calendar open at the time.

When you press **OK** a music symbol will be shown to the left of the appointment and a length bar will have been placed to the right of the times, showing the duration of the entry.

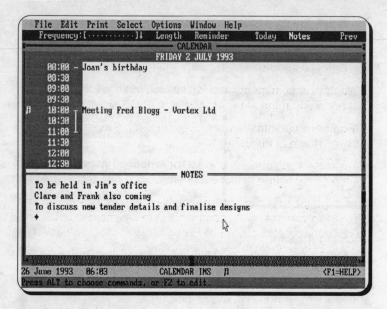

Using a Note Pane:

One line per appointment does not give you much room to enter detailed information into your calendar. This is no problem because, as shown above, you can make extra notes by opening a Notes pane. The easiest way to do this is with the Toolbar **Notes** option, otherwise use the **Options**, **Show Notes** toggle switch. Every appointments page can have its own Notes pane.

You can change the size of the pane by dragging its top border up, or down, the screen. As we shall see later you can print your notes with their appointments schedule, to give you hard copy.

Types of Appointments:

By default, an appointment is considered to be an Only Once type. The Calendar handles six types of appointments though and you can easily convert between them.

An **Only Once** type is, as the name suggests, placed in the calendar only once, on the day that it was entered.

A **Daily** appointment is entered at the same time on every day of the week.

124

A **Weekday** type is entered at the same time on every day of the usual working week (not Saturdays and Sundays). If you are working in a Muslim calendar country this one will present problems!

Weekly appointments are scheduled on the same day of every week at the same time.

Monthly appointments are scheduled on the same date of every month at the same time.

A **Yearly** appointment is ideal for birthdays as it places the entry on the same day of every year.

To change an appointment type, highlight the entry and use the **Edit**, **Appointment** menu command. A faster method is to click the down arrow to the right of **Frequency** on the Toolbar. This opens the drop-down menu shown below:

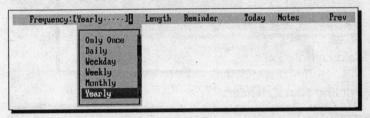

Click on one of the menu options to select it, or drag the highlight down the menu, with the left mouse button depressed and release it when the required selection is highlighted.

Toolbar Options:
The above shows all the Calendar Toolbar options, most of which should be fairly familiar to you, if you have been working through this with the program on. If not, the meanings of the Toolbar options are as follows:

Option	*Result*
Frequency: [ ]↓	Change frequency setting, as above
Length	Change appointment length
Reminder	Switch a reminder on, or off
Today	Jump the display to current date
Notes	Toggle the Notes pane on, or off
Prev	Print preview the current page(s).

The Appointment Box:

To quickly review, or change, all the details of a particular appointment, double click your mouse on its line, but to the left of the time bar. Without a mouse, you would use the **Edit**, **Appointment** menu command. The following box opens, which lists all the properties of the selected appointment. It is an easy matter to change any of these, if required.

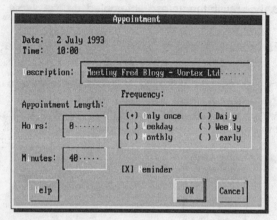

Printing your Calendar:

The **Print**, **Print** command will activate the print facility. Before printing your calendar, you should preview it on the screen to check what will actually print. This is best done with the Toolbar **Prev** option, which opens the Preview box shown below:

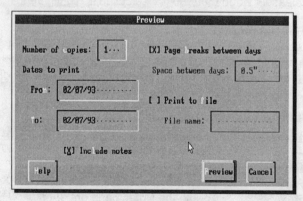

The **Dates to print** boxes will both be set to the current appointment date. Make changes here, depending on the pages you want to commit to paper. By default, Works will print calendar pages on separate sheets. If this is not what you want, clear the **Page breaks between days** box. Select **Include notes** and press the **Preview** button (or the <Alt+P> keys).

A useful schedule of each selected days appointments should be printed out, with the notes entries placed below.

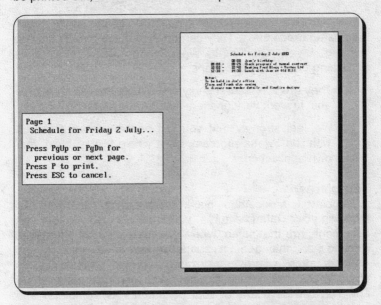

If the display is acceptable simply press **P** to print it to paper.

If the text formatting of the calendar material needs changing, press <Esc> to return to the Calendar screen and use the settings contained in the **Print**, **Font & Style** dialogue box to reformat both the Appointments and the Notes entries.

WorksWizards

With WorksWizards, which are new to Version 3.0, you get step-by-step assistance in creating particular types of Works documents. There are WorksWizards set up for creating an address book database, personalised form letters, mailing labels, a Data Finder and a File Finder. WorksWizards are produced by Microsoft and, unlike macros, cannot be 'home made'.

To start a WorksWizard when you start Works, choose the WorksWizards button in the initial Startup dialogue box. Select the WorksWizard you want and then press the **OK** button.

To start a WorksWizard when you are already using Works, use the **File**, **WorksWizard** command and again select the WorksWizard you want and then press the **OK** button.

We strongly recommend you experiment with these automated procedures. They can often produce the results you want in a very short time. We have not spent much time explaining them for two reasons:

1. They are very user friendly and almost anyone should be able to work through them without any problems.

2. We feel strongly that you will become more proficient with the Works program, as a whole, if you build your own applications.

Templates

A Template is a document 'blank' which can contain titles, text, formatting and other features, which do not change between documents of the same type. You can open a Template, rename it and then adapt it to whatever you need.

Works comes with over a dozen pre-formed templates, some of which you may find useful, and some you most certainly will not. You can save any of your documents as Templates and use them in the same way.

We will step through an example of how to use a Template. Select **Create New File**, either from the opening screen dialogue box, or from the **File** menu. The box opened is shown on page 9, if you cannot remember what it looks like. Select **Word Processor,** if necessary, but it should be the default.

We have so far not used the section on the right of this box which is headed **Available Templates**. It contains a listing of all the Word Processing Templates provided with Works. Select **Office Memo** which produces a paper heading suitable for sending memo notes around an office complex (or wherever).

Try **Print**, **Preview** to see what the document actually looks like. You could now customise this Template, maybe with your company name, your own name, date formats, etc., and then save it. To make it into an ordinary document use the **File**, **Save As** command, so that you can change its name from WORD1.

If you want it to continue as a Template check the **Save as Template** box. This facility should prove very useful for making Templates not only from your documents, but from spreadsheets and databases.

* * *

Works has more commands and functions which can be used to build and run your applications in special ways. What this book has tried to do is to introduce you to the overall subject and give the beginner a solid foundation on which to build future knowledge.

* * *

APPENDIX A - FUNCTIONS

Microsoft Work's =functions are built-in formulae that perform specialised calculations in both spreadsheets and databases. Their general format is:

=name(arg1,arg2,...)

where 'name' is the function name, and 'arg1', 'arg2', etc, are the arguments required for the evaluation of the function. Arguments must appear in a parenthesized list as shown above and their exact number depends on the function being used. However, there are seven functions that do not require arguments and are used with empty parentheses. These are: =ERR( ), =FALSE( ), =NA( ), =NOW( ), =PI( ), =RAND( ) and =TRUE( ).

There are two types of arguments used with =functions: numeric values and range values, the type used being dependent on the type of function. Numeric value arguments can be entered either directly as numbers, as a cell address, a cell range name or as a formula. Range value arguments can be entered either as a range address or a range name.

Types of Functions

There are several types of functions, such as mathematical, logical, financial, statistical, date and time, special and, new to Version 3.0, text. Each type requires their own number and type of arguments. These are listed below under the various function categories.

Mathematical Functions:

Mathematical functions evaluate a result using numeric arguments. The various functions and their meaning are as follows:

Function	Description
=ABS(X)	Returns the absolute value of X
=ACOS(X)	Returns the angle in radians, whose cosine is X (arc cos of X)
=ASIN(X)	Returns the angle in radians, whose sine is X (arc sin of X)

=ATAN(X)	Returns the angle in radians, between Pi/2 and –Pi/2, whose tangent is X (arc tan of X – 2 quadrant)
=ATAN2(X,Y)	Returns the angle in radians, between Pi and –Pi whose tangent is Y/X (arc tan of Y/X – 4 quadrant)
=COS(X)	Returns the cosine of angle X, (X must be in radians)
=EXP(X)	Raises e to the power of X
=INT(X)	Returns the integer part of X
=LN(X)	Returns the natural logarithm (base e) of X
=LOG(X)	Returns the logarithm (base 10) of X
=MOD(X,Y)	Returns the remainder of X/Y
=PI( )	Returns the value of Pi (3.141593)
=RAND( )	Returns a random number between 0 and 1, but excluding 1
=ROUND(X,N)	Returns the value of X rounded to N places
=SIN(X)	Returns the sine of angle X (X must be in radians)
=SQRT(X)	Returns the square root of X
=TAN(X)	Returns the tangent of angle X (X must be in radians).

Logical Functions:

Logical functions produce a value based on the result of a conditional statement, using numeric arguments. The various functions and their meanings are as follows:

Function	*Description*
=AND(Arg0,Arg1,..)	Returns 1 (TRUE) if all arguments are true, else returns 0 (FALSE)
=FALSE( )	Returns the logical value 0
=IF(Cr,X,Y)	Returns the value X if Cr is TRUE and Y if Cr is FALSE
=ISERR(X)	Returns 1 (TRUE) if X contains ERR, else returns 0 (FALSE)
=ISNA(X)	Returns 1 (TRUE) if X contains N/A, else returns 0 (FALSE)

=OR*(Arg0,Arg1,..)*	Returns 1 (TRUE) if any argument is true, else returns 0 (FALSE)
=NOT(Arg)	Reverses the logic of Arg
=TRUE( )	Returns the logical value 1.

Financial Functions:

Financial functions evaluate loans, annuities, and cash flows over a period of time, using numeric arguments. The various functions and their meaning are as follows:

Function	*Description*
=CTERM(Rt,Fv,Pv)	Returns the number of compounding periods for an investment of present value Pv, to grow to a future value Fv, at a fixed interest rate Rt
=DDB(Ct,Sg,Lf,Pd)	Returns the double-declining depreciation allowance of an asset, given the original cost Ct, predicted salvage value Sg, the life Lf of the asset, and the period Pd
=FV(Pt,Rt,Tm)	Returns the future value of a series of equal payments, each of equal amount Pt, earning a periodic interest rate Rt, over a number of payment periods in term Tm
=IRR(Gs,Rg)	Returns the internal rate of return of the series of cash flows in a range Rg, based on the approximate percentage guess Gs of the IRR
=NPV(Rt,Rg)	Returns the present value of the series of future cash flows in range Rg, discounted at a periodic interest rate Rt
=PMT(Pl,Rt,Tm)	Returns the amount of the periodic payment needed to pay off the principal Pl, at a periodic interest rate Rt, over the number of payment periods in term Tm
=PV(Pt,Rt,Tm)	Returns the present value of a series of equal payments, each of equal amount Pt, discounted at a periodic

133

	interest rate Rt, over a number of payment periods in term Tm
=RATE(Fv,Pv,Tm)	Returns the periodic interest rate necessary for a present value Pv to grow to a future value Fv, over the number of compounding periods in term Tm
=SLN(Ct,Sg,Lf)	Returns the straight-line depreciation allowance of an asset for one period, given the original cost Ct, predicted salvage value Sg, and the life Lf of the asset
=SYD(Ct,Sg,Lf,Pd)	Returns the sum-of-the-years' digits depreciation allowance of an asset, given the original cost Ct, predicted salvage value Sg, the life Lf of the asset, and the period Pd
=TERM(Pt,Rt,Fv)	Returns the number of payment periods of an investment, given the amount of each payment Pt, the periodic interest rate Rt, and the future value of the investment Fv.

Statistical Functions:

Statistical functions evaluate lists of values using numeric arguments or cell ranges. The various functions and their meaning are as follows:

Function	*Description*
=AVG(Rg0,Rg1,..)	Returns the average of values in range(s) Rg0, Rg1,...
=COUNT(Rg0,Rg1,..)	Returns the number of non-blank entries in range(s) Rg0, Rg1,..
=MAX(Rg0,Rg1,..)	Returns the maximum value in range(s) Rg0, Rg1,..
=MIN(Rg0,Rg1,..)	Returns the minimum value in range(s) Rg0, Rg1,..
=STD(Rg0,Rg1,..)	Returns the standard deviation of values in range(s) Rg0, Rg1,..
=SUM(Rg0,Rg1,..)	Returns the sum of values in range(s) Rg0, Rg1,..

=VAR(Rg0,Rg1,..)   Returns the variance of values in
                        range(s) Rg0, Rg1,..

Date and Time Functions:
Date and time functions generate and use serial numbers to
represent dates and times. Each date between 1 January, 1900
and 31 December 2099 has an integer serial number starting
with 1 and ending with 73050. Each moment during a day has a
decimal serial number starting with 0.000 at midnight and
ending with 0.99999 just before the following midnight. Thus the
value 0.5 indicates midday. The various functions and their
meanings are as follows:

Function	*Description*
=DATE(Yr,Mh,Dy)	Returns the date number of Yr,Mh,Dy
=DAY(Dn)	Returns the day number of date number Dn
=HOUR(Tn)	Returns the hour number of time number Tn
=MINUTE(Tn)	Returns the minute number of time number Tn
=MONTH(Dn)	Returns the month number of date number Dn
=NOW( )	Returns the serial number for the current date and time
=SECOND(Tn)	Returns the second number of time number Tn
=TIME(Hr,Ms,Ss)	Returns the time number of Hr,Ms,Ss
=YEAR(Dn)	Returns the year number of date number Dn.

Special Functions:
Special functions perform a variety of advanced tasks, such as
looking up a value in a table. The various functions and their
meaning are as follows:

Function	*Description*
=CHOOSE(X,V0,..,Vn)	Returns the Xth value in the list V0,..,Vn

=COLS(Rg)	Returns the number of columns in the range Rg
=ERR( )	Returns the value of ERR
=HLOOKUP(X,Rg,Rn)	Performs a horizontal table look-up by comparing the value X to each cell in the top row, or index row, in range Rg, then moves down the column in which a match is found by the specified row number Rn
=INDEX(Rg,Cn,Rw)	Returns the value of the cell in range at the intersection of column Cn and row Rw
=NA( )	Returns the numeric value of N/A
=ROWS(Rg)	Returns the number of rows in range Rg
=VLOOKUP(X,Rg,Cn)	Performs a vertical table look-up by comparing the value X to each cell in the first column, or index column, in range Rg, then moves across the row in which a match is found by the specified column number Cn.

Text Functions:

Text functions operate on strings in databases and spreadsheets and produce numeric or string values, dependent on the function. If you include text in the formula statement it must be enclosed in quotation marks (").

Function	*Description*
=EXACT(Sg1,Sg2)	Returns 1 (TRUE) if strings Sg1 and Sg2 are exactly alike, otherwise 0 (FALSE)
=FIND(Ss,Sg,Sn)	Returns position at which the first occurrence of search string Ss begins in string Sg, starting the search from search number Sn
=LEFT(Sg,N)	Returns the first (leftmost) N characters in string Sg
=LENGTH(Sg)	Returns the number of characters in string Sg

=LOWER(Sg)	Returns all lowercase letters in string Sg
=MID(Sg,Sn,N)	Returns N characters from string Sg beginning with the character at Sn
=N(Rg)	Returns the numeric value in the upper left corner cell in range Rg
=PROPER(Sg)	Returns all words in string Sg with first letter in uppercase and the rest in lowercase
=REPEAT(Sg,N)	Returns string Sg N times
=REPLACE(O,S,N,Ns)	Removes N characters from original string O, starting at character S and then inserts new string Ns in the vacated place
=RIGHT(Sg,N)	Returns the last (rightmost) N characters in string Sg
=S(Rg)	Returns the string value in the upper left corner cell in range Rg
=STRING(X,N)	Returns the numeric value X as a string, with N decimal places
=TRIM(Sg)	Returns string Sg with no leading, trailing or contiguous spaces
=UPPER(Sg)	Returns all letters in string Sg in uppercase
=VALUE(Sg)	Returns the numeric value of string Sg.

INDEX

142

COMPANION DISC TO THIS BOOK

This book contains many pages of file/program listings. There is no reason why you should spend hours typing them into your computer, unless you wish to do so, or need the practice.

The COMPANION DISC for this book comes with all the example listings. It is available in both 3.5-inch and 5.25-inch formats.

COMPANION DISCS for all books written by the same author(s) and published by BERNARD BABANI (publishing), are also available and are listed at the front of this book. Make sure you specify the BP book number and the book title in your order.

ORDERING INSTRUCTIONS

To obtain your copy of the companion disc, fill-in the order form below, enclose a cheque (payable to **P.R.M. Oliver)** or a postal order, and send it to the address given below.

Book No.	Book Name	Unit Price	Total Price
BP ___		£3.50	
BP ___		£3.50	
BP ___		£3.50	
Name .... Address		Sub-total	£.............
		P & P (@ 45p/disc)	£.............
		Total Due	£.............
Disc Format 3.5-inch....... 5.25-inch.......			
Send to: P.R.M. Oliver, CSM, Pool, Redruth, Cornwall, TR15 3SE			